# SELF MASTERY

# SELF MASTERY

Through Integration of Spirit, Body and Mind

Penny Weaver

Copyright © 2002 by Penny Weaver.

Library of Congress Number: 2002090257
ISBN :      Hardcover    1-4010-4603-7
            Softcover    1-4010-4602-9

All rights reserved. No part of this book may be reproduced or transmitted in any form or by any means, electronic or mechanical, including photocopying, recording, or by any information storage and retrieval system, without permission in writing from the copyright owner.

This book was printed in the United States of America.

**To order additional copies of this book, contact:**
Xlibris Corporation
1-888-795-4274
www.Xlibris.com
Orders@Xlibris.com

# CONTENTS

Acknowledgements .................................................................. 9
Foreword ................................................................................ 11
Introduction .......................................................................... 15

PART I CONCEPTS OF SELF MASTERY ........................... 21
  1   What is Integration Psychology? ......................................... 23
  2   Starting the Journey ............................................................ 25
  3   The Flow of Self Mastery .................................................... 30
  4   Important Components of the Self ...................................... 34
  5   Meditation ........................................................................... 39
        *Chakras* ............................................................................ 42
        *Energy* ............................................................................. 45
        *Sekhem-Seichim-Reiki* .................................................... 46
        *The Meditation Process* .................................................. 47
        *Physical Changes* ........................................................... 50
        *Zen and Living in the Moment* ....................................... 52
        *Keys to Success with Meditation* .................................... 53
  6   Empower Your Work with Ethics ........................................ 55

PART II TOOLS AND TECHNIQUES TO
ENHANCE YOUR EXPERIENCES ......................................... 61
  7   Mind Mapping .................................................................... 63
  8   Journaling ........................................................................... 66
  9   Pendulum Power ................................................................. 71
 10  Aura Viewing ...................................................................... 76
 11  Time .................................................................................... 80
 12  Affirmations and Self-Hypnosis .......................................... 82
 13  Circles ................................................................................. 87

## PART III ADVANCED TECHNIQUES .................................. 97

14   Mystical Experiences .............................................. 99
     *Goddess Energy* ................................................. 100
     *Fairy Realm* ..................................................... 103
     *Spirit Guides* .................................................... 106
     *Sacred Sites* .................................................... 108
     *Grokking* ........................................................ 108
15   Past Life Experiences ........................................... 112
16   Parts of Yourself .................................................. 116

## PART IV SELF MASTERY THROUGH INTEGRATION ........ 123

17   Healing and Manifesting on the Astral Plane ..................... 125
18   Integration Psychology ......................................... 137

Bibliography ............................................................. 143
Index ...................................................................... 145

This book is dedicated to the health, happiness and positive evolution of humanity.

# ACKNOWLEDGEMENTS

With the greatest of gratitude, respect, love and appreciation, I, Penny Weaver, thank my adorable soul mate and husband, Howard, my magical and dedicated parents Joan and Jack Chaille', my many wondrous and caring mentors and in particular, Dr. Robert Fink, all the clinicians and therapists who have served me, my amazing and intriguing family members, Howard's endearing family members, each and every one of the clients I have served, our spiritual guides, our ascended masters, my fascinating friends and amazing medical practitioners who have created healings for me and my loved ones. I thank the planet Earth herself. I thank the town of Northville, Michigan and all the people in it for their nurturance. I will forever be grateful for the relationship and friendship with Peggy Campbell who has listened and corroborated on the many adventures that we have created together. I thank the Divine Source, whom I call God. May God bless us all and guide us to peace and health.

I, Peggy Campbell, would like to thank my supportive, loving and resourceful husband, Ron, through whom all things are possible. Also love and appreciation goes to my family, Ron's family and the friends who are the lights of our lives. I thank my sister Barbara Schoen for continually inspiring me. And from the bottom of my heart, thanks to Penny Weaver for showing me the way and providing the opportunity to do all the things I love.

## Credits

Peg Campbell, Writer
Linda Detherage, Editor
Sharon Irla, Cover Design
Steve McMath, Illustrations
Jeannie Nelson, Editor
Kathleen Thompson, Photographs

# FOREWORD

When Penny invited me to collaborate on writing this book with her, I immediately said yes because it was the fulfillment of one of my dreams. I've always wanted to write a book and this was not only an opportunity to do that but also a chance to help others find happiness.

I have 15 years experience in marketing and public relations. After decades in corporate life, I began living my dream when I started Campbell Communications, my own marketing and public relations firm. Throughout my career I've spearheaded marketing/promotional campaigns and major events of numerous varieties. I've designed and edited magazines, newsletters and booklets, and written magazine articles, white papers and newspaper articles. I've designed a multitude of web sites. But none of these projects compares to the sense of satisfaction and accomplishment I've achieved in working with Penny Weaver on this book to share her ideas with others.

I met Penny when she asked me to design a web site for her practice. The more I learned about Penny and her unique practice, the more fascinated I became. Penny contracted with me to be her marketing agent and we discovered that we had a dynamic, synergistic relationship. As I worked with her to develop a promotional strategy for her practice, I was extremely impressed with the way she positively touched and transformed so many peoples' lives. Using what Penny coined Integration

Psychology, she combined and personalized traditional psychological practices with ancient metaphysical techniques to develop a unique form of therapy. Penny's clients learned to overcome blocks, become masters of their destinies, manifest their hopes and dreams and live in peace, joy and abundance.

Penny's credentials include a master's degree in guidance and counseling, a specialist degree in psychology and a master's degree in business. She has been a practicing limited licensed psychologist (LLP) since 1988. A Michigan LLP permits practice under the supervision of a Michigan licensed psychologist.

Prior to entering the field of psychology, Penny had many diverse experiences including being a flight attendant and vice-president for sales and marketing in the private school industry. She worked in a rehabilitation center for patients with traumatic brain damage, a university mental health clinic and a hospital inpatient and outpatient setting before establishing her private practice. She now sees clients on an individual basis, and teaches and mentors clinicians, psychics, healers, business people and others from all walks of life.

The therapeutic techniques she synthesized evolved during the 22,000 hours she spent individually in sessions with people. These hours in therapy were spent with her clients searching, documenting and accounting for universal truth.

Penny now practices as a limited licensed psychologist and certified hypnotherapist. She is a Reiki master teacher, Sekhem-Seichim master teacher and does work with past life regression. Penny teaches classes in meditation (beginning through advanced), Reiki (Reiki I through Master), Sekhem-Seichim (Level I through Master Teacher), astral travel, and self mastery through the integration of the mind, body and spirit. Penny's most recent adventures include leading spiritual sojourns throughout the country.

Penny is appreciative of the work of psychologist Carl Jung who identified and utilized the metaphysical principles and the all-knowing unconscious. She believes his work has been instrumental in helping her to work with people to achieve their hopes and dreams. When people make their unconscious become conscious and then tap into the all-knowing unconscious of human beings, they can have complete power over their lives.

I was eager to jump in when Penny told me of her plan to write this book and share with others the therapies she has brought together. Since beginning the work on this book, I have incorporated meditation into my daily life, used the techniques listed here and found my life greatly enhanced.

The book fuses ancient practices with the new age/metaphysical techniques and therapies Penny utilizes in her clinical practice. Now she wants to share the success secrets with others. This book resonates with the truths that can assist in your success and empower you to achieve the potential you have within yourself. I know you will attain the same sense of satisfaction and success I have found in following Penny's map for success.

Peg Campbell

# INTRODUCTION

The purpose of this book is to share with others the positive discoveries Penny Weaver has made through the practice of Integration Psychology. Many people have transformed themselves to become whom they desire to be by learning to listen to their highest selves. The book is aimed at two primary audiences.

First, the book is written to help you experience a fulfilled life on earth by evolving spiritually, personally and professionally. You may seek assistance with only one of these aspects of your life or you may work on all three. What generally happens is that these three components develop simultaneously and synergistically when using Integration Psychology and the methods outlined in this book.

Second, the book is written to share with other therapists the truths and techniques Penny discovered during her years of work. The intent is for other therapists to use them in their practices.

The end goal is the same: To help people utilize the integrative methods that will help them vision and manifest their dreams and reach their highest potentials. Through the integrative process, individuals can achieve a sense of empowerment and realize and fulfill their destinies. This fulfillment can be achieved under any circumstance. Especially in the most dire of situations, these methods have and will work to create the best possible outcomes.

## Note to Professionals

Although the metaphysical concepts and practices discussed in this book may not necessarily appear to have a place in traditional therapy, they can be excellent tools to help clients become more focused on the work they are doing under your guidance. These methods are designed to help increase awareness, sensitivity and insight—and should not conflict with most therapeutic practices.

## How to Use this Book

This self-help book is designed to assess your needs and develop a plan of action. It is written in a simple, straightforward manner and can be read in an afternoon. Review it to get an idea of what is offered. Then go back and use it as a workbook by following the steps suggested and practicing the exercises as outlined. There is a tremendous amount of information available on the topics touched on here and you are encouraged to seek more information for further study.

For efficiency of use, the book is divided into four parts. Many chapters contain exercises and you are strongly encouraged to complete them because they will enhance your understanding of the material and your ability to master the techniques. The exercises will also help you incorporate the message and meaning into your life.

***Part I – Concepts of Self Mastery***—This section relates the basic information about Integration Psychology. It outlines the four fundamentals to get you in touch with yourself so you can achieve your hopes and dreams. This is accomplished by:

- Understanding your highest self, ego and feelings
- Meditating
- Communicating with your highest self
- Practicing the highest ethics

**Part II – *Tools and Techniques to Enhance Your Experiences*** —This section offers several enhancements to meditation to help you communicate with your highest self. It is a resource that you can tap into at any point to help achieve your goals.

The tools include creating a mind map, journaling, using a pendulum, viewing auras, manipulating time, using affirmations and self-hypnosis, and symbols and circles.

**Part III – *Advanced Techniques*** —This section contains some advanced techniques and information. Once you begin meditating and using some of the techniques suggested, you may begin to have mystical experiences. Part III outlines communication with goddess and fairy energy, spirit guides and visiting sacred sites. It discusses past life regression and parts of yourself.

**Part IV   *Self Mastery Through Integration*** —The final part integrates the topics discussed in this book by helping you understand co-creation, the six dimensions, healing and manifesting on the astral plane and integration.

While the material is presented in a linear format, the fact of the matter is that the information is more circular than linear. That is, one part may be related to another but not necessarily in a contiguous format. You can use the information by going through it chapter by chapter. Or, read Part I which will provide you with a solid base of information to help you connect to your highest self. Then go through Part II picking and choosing the techniques that appeal most to you. For more advanced information, go through Part III. Finally, use Part IV as a final step to integration and self mastery.

It is very helpful while going through this information to engage in additional therapy or training. Alternative and traditional services are often utilized. Some of the services people have found beneficial include:

- Hypnosis
- Psychotherapy
- Massage therapy (traditional massage or reflexology)
- Reiki-Sekhem-Seichim
- Past life therapy
- Classes or coaching
- Classes in meditation
- Physical workouts (Yoga, Pilates, exercise or weights)
- Chiropractic
- Acupuncture

This is only a partial list and progress can occur much more quickly if you participate in therapy, classes or coaching that stimulate the mental, emotional, physical or spiritual levels of yourself.

The ultimate goal is to co-create. Co-creation means listening to your highest self and following through on the guidance and actions suggested. When you do this, you bring the Divine to earth and into your life.

Think about the difference between two people you know. Bring to mind someone you know who always experiences problems and troubles in whatever is going on in his life or whatever he attempts to do. Then bring to mind another person you know who accomplishes things and is happy with life. Most likely the difference between the two is that the successful individual has learned to live in the flow of Divine energy and to be aware of guidance for the fulfillment of hopes, dreams and destiny.

In this process of flow and connection, spiritual energy channeled from the source of love and earth energy are combined and used for the greatest outcome of activation of free will and actualizing destiny. The world is transforming and many people such as you are looking for something different right now. Once you have learned to connect with your highest self, the stars and ancestors, you can return to your roots by becoming more telepathic, cooperative and realizing the unity of all things.

This book is intended to benefit the reader's knowledge. Any reader needing medical, mental, emotional, spiritual or physical assistance is advised to contact a professional practitioner.

# PART I

# Concepts of Self Mastery

# CHAPTER 1

## *What is Integration Psychology?*

In the evolution of psychology, Integration Psychology can be considered the ultimate step to self-fulfillment. Integration Psychology allows you to become the master of your destiny. The process outlined in this book enables you to go beyond your issues; develop a connection with your highest self; and formulate a plan for your spiritual evolution, personal growth and professional development. By reaching your full potential and achieving your purpose in life, you can make your hopes and dreams a reality. This brings peace, love and harmony to you and those around you.

At the dawn of the new millennium, Integrated Psychology takes an eclectic approach to personal development by combining the best of and most successful therapies from traditional and contemporary psychology as well as the arts and methods from ancient, esoteric wisdom. It's an adventure in self-discovery and transformation through a cornucopia of traditions, practices and religious doctrines. These methods are meant to interface with organized religion and not be in conflict with it. In merging truths from the past with contemporary therapies, you can rediscover and utilize the supernatural powers possessed by the ancients. This redefined combination emphasizes the model of abundance, absence of fear and the premise that we are not here to suffer but to experience life to its fullest while on the earth plane.

Individuals encompass four levels—the mental, emotional, physical and spiritual. In meditation these can be integrated. Through this integration a different spirituality is emerging. Its focus is on living in the moment and connecting to one's highest self. Many medical specialists and scientists are now realizing the mind, body and spirit connection and its role in maximizing mental, spiritual and physical health. This new spirituality, connecting to one's highest self and effectively utilizing all the energies that are available, is the basis of Integration Psychology.

As your energy stream changes through meditation, you have the opportunity to tap into your highest self and connect to the Divine Source. Exactly what the Divine Source means is open to your interpretation, be it the Creator, God, Goddess, unconditional love or whatever name you choose. Within the energy stream of the Divine (referred to as Divine white light, chi, ki, qi, prana and a variety of other names) is where we find abundance—the abundance of health, love, and prosperity.

Integration Psychology serves as a roadmap to guide you through your journey. And like a roadmap, there are different ways to reach the final destination. The travel may be a short trip, a series of short trips or a continuous journey. The route selected depends on your starting point, where you have previously been, current conditions and your spiritual purpose. No matter how the process unfolds, you will discover a new sense of empowerment that will lead you to the realization of your highest vision for yourself.

# CHAPTER 2

## *Starting the Journey*

We are on earth at this time for two reasons and this book is written to help you understand and fulfill them. First, each person has his or her own Divine mission and reason for being here. Second, people are also here to channel and share love, peace and harmony on the earth. So, no matter what we do, it needs to be done with love, peace and harmony or we defeat the purpose of our existence. The challenge is to rise to the occasion and to deal with the lessons we need to learn while bringing in love, peace and harmony.

You have taken a big step in moving forward with your work to connect with your highest self and ultimately become the master of your destiny and live your hopes and dreams. While no one can tell you what to think or do, this book can guide you by providing the tools and techniques to let you discover your own personal truths and knowings. What you will learn comes primarily from inside you, from your experiences and from wisdom gained by connecting to your highest self.

For many people, the beginning of the journey is marked with some sort of significant life or emotional experience. The experience may be something that is very painful or life threatening. Or it can be the realization that life is not what you think it should be. Or it can be that you feel you have a lot of potential but just don't know how to activate it. The search for meaning in one's existence is a powerful drive and motivation that demands to be fulfilled.

## Spirituality in the US in the New Millennium

We are on the brink of some very powerful changes taking place in this country and this is a great time to be on earth. In ancient times people had to go to temples to feel compassion and love. Today we find that we have evolved to the point where we have the capacity to generate our own compassion, empathy, balance and harmony from wherever we are.

The new spirituality is emerging and integrating naturally. Through communication with our highest selves, we are enhancing our mental and physical health and channeling more prosperity into our lives and relationships.

We often experience some similar, common situations called universal truths. At the heart or core of an idea or issue is a universal truth. A universal truth is something that is true for most people and has a vibration that most of us resonate to.

## Belief vs. Knowing

You are on a voyage to discover yourself. This can be done effectively if you work with facts and the concrete truths about yourself, not the beliefs you have about things and yourself. Understanding that most beliefs have been laid down by forces outside yourself (your culture, your parents, your teachers, and such) is a good place to start uncovering the core truths that exist inside you. These truths have been with you always, and simply need to be uncovered by peeling away what is not really spoken in your own voice or heard in your own soul.

The mind is very powerful and you can influence what happens in your life by what you believe. Sometimes our thoughts and beliefs block our vision. Your beliefs about yourself and others are outwardly reflected and manifested in your outer life. This shows in every aspect of your life including your body, career and relationships.

You have the power to get beyond your beliefs, gain truth and as a result, change your entire life. Meditation enhances this process. If things are happening in your life that you do not like, ask yourself why they are happening and how you can change them.

When you begin to understand your missions and purposes more clearly, many possibilities and options begin to unfold and become known to you. Meditation will connect you to your own personal knowing. Knowing is much more efficient and powerful than belief.

## Where Are You Now?

As mentioned earlier, many people get on the path because of a significant life or emotional experience. Or it could be that your life is rolling along, with no major complaints but something raises questions. Let's take a look and see if you can identify yourself in any of these situations. Do any of these situations arise in your life?

- Do you spend time asking "What am I here for? What am I supposed to do with my life?"
- Do you ask yourself, "Is that all there is?" While successful professionally, you may not feel like what you have really achieved is your

life's goals nor do you really know what they are.
- Do you wonder about the meaning of your life?
- Did a near-death experience change the way you think about your life?
- Do you feel you're ready to move into a future that makes great things happen, yet you don't know how or what?
- Do you experience irrational fears that are not based in the rationality of your life?

Or do you feel:

- Depressed? With feelings of hopelessness, helplessness, despair?
- Trapped? With feelings of hopelessness, loneliness, no way out?
- Addicted? Using substances or behaviors to mask and avoid pain and emotions?
- Frustrated? Knowing there is more to life but don't know how to access it?
- Victimized? Do other people take advantage of you?
- Anxious? With fears you can't identify?
- Jealous, bitter or resentful? With feelings of dissatisfaction with your own life as well as feelings of scarcity and competition?

If you are experiencing any of the feelings or situations, this book will help you identify what you need to do and how to do it in order to live your hopes and dreams.

## Where Do You Want to Be?

The key to integration and achieving success is being connected to your Divine purposes and callings. Your Divine purposes and callings brought you to the earth in the first place and beg to be acted upon.

The seeds of knowledge about your Divine purposes are in your dreams (day and night), fantasies, and secret hopes about how you want to live. Activate this information by beginning to remember what you daydreamed about when you were around the age of 10 or 11 years old. Take some time alone to think about this and remember.

It's often said in our culture today that each of us came to the earth after having made an agreement with the Divine Source about the purpose of our existence and the lessons we will learn. The challenge of these lessons is supposed to help us gain strength to transform and transmute our energy to the vibration of love. By going through this process, we bring in more love, light and a higher vibration to the earth.

When you are on the path to carrying out your Divine mission, you are more integrated, whole, focused, satisfied and accomplished. When you are channeling love and light, you are tapped into unlimited potential and receive abundance. This can be abundance of love, prosperity, career opportunities, relationships or whatever you manifest in your life.

# CHAPTER 3

## *The Flow of Self Mastery*

You are reading this book because you wish to achieve self mastery. Self mastery is an ascension process. Perhaps the easiest way to describe it is to say it is a circular process. Chapter 13 discusses the significance of the circular shape with one phase merging into the next and then beginning again. The circle is a good metaphor to describe the ascension process in the flow of self mastery because the phases do merge. As you work, you will find that the journey is not always smooth and unidirectional. Until we gain mastery or learn our lessons, we overlap, reach a plateau and feel blocked.

It's easier to understand the ascension process if you break down the process into several components. Diagram 1 outlines the process as follows.

**Phase 1:** *Begin and take action*—This is where it starts. As explained, something prompts the beginning of the self-mastery process. It may be a life crisis, emotional experience or recognition of the need or desire to change. It can be major or minor but it inspires you to do something about your situation. This desire can be enhanced by individual therapy, further investigation and research through things such as taking a class, reading a book or engaging in a new workout routine.

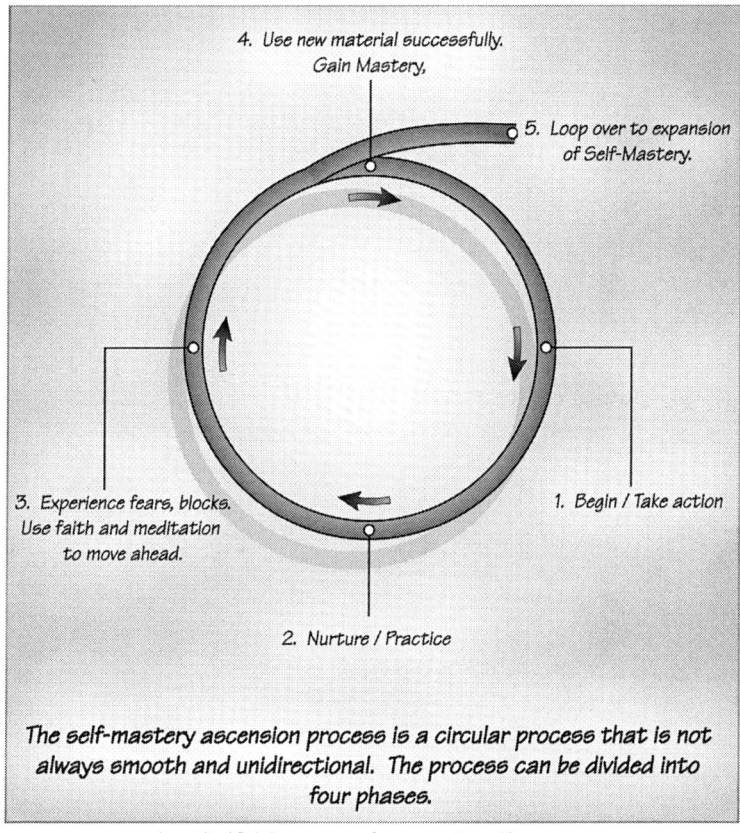

The self-mastery ascension process is a circular process that is not always smooth and unidirectional. The process can be divided into four phases.

1 – Self-Mastery Ascension Process

**Phase 2:** *Nurture and practice*—Encouragement of the changes desired needs to take place. Practice new techniques by using the chosen tools in Parts II and III of the book to help make changes. The more you learn and incorporate changes, the easier and quicker the process becomes.

**Phase 3:** *Fears, doubts, mystery and unknown*—Sometimes these threaten a person and that makes this the most difficult segment to get through. To excel at something, a person must address and work through blocks. Often the blocks are hidden. It is in this phase that one's worst fears and blocks are discovered. Use faith and meditation to move ahead. You can ask to be given the easiest lesson to be learned.

Practice helps overcome fears and doubts. Imagine yourself stepping into the center of the circle. Put yourself in the center of your life; be with yourself in this process and you will feel more centered and experience less of the erratic ups and downs that often take place in dealing with fears, doubts, mystery and the unknown.

**Phase 4:** *Gain mastery*—It is here that you can successfully incorporate new material, ideas and ultimately gain mastery of your life. Mastery is achieved through experience, rigor, repetition, nurturance and inside and outside advice.

Now let's break the process down.

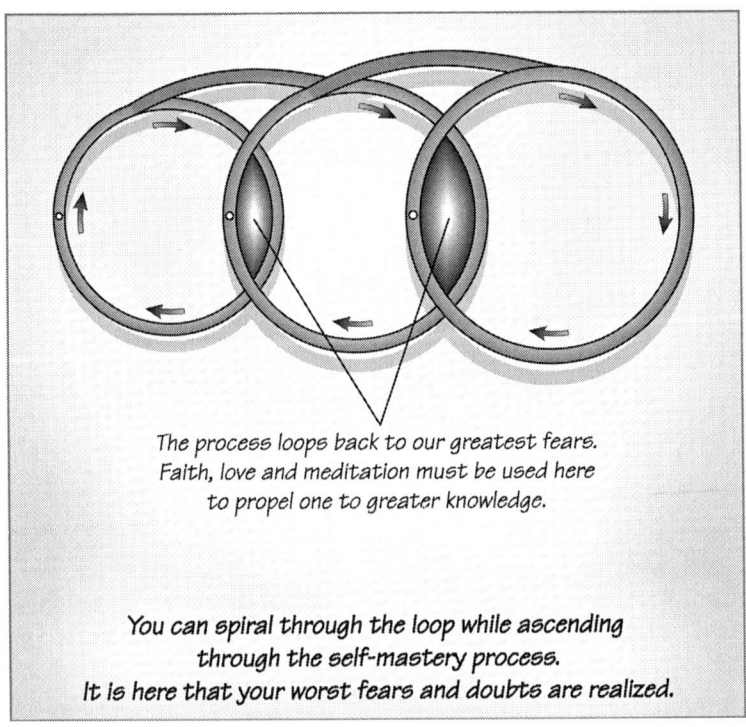

The process loops back to our greatest fears. Faith, love and meditation must be used here to propel one to greater knowledge.

You can spiral through the loop while ascending through the self-mastery process.
It is here that your worst fears and doubts are realized.

2 – Self-Mastery Loop Process

The flow of self mastery has a motion and resembles a spiral as indicated in Diagram 2. It is in the overlapping edges where the process loops back, as indicated in the self-mastery loop process diagram, where you realize your fears and doubts. It is here that faith, love and meditation must be used to propel you to greater knowledge.

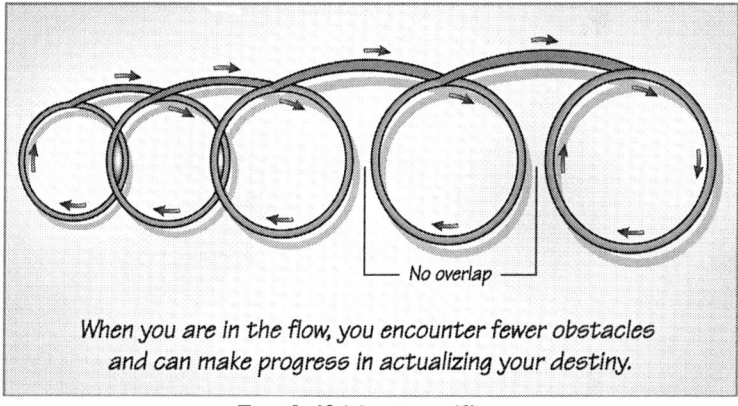

3 – Self-Mastery Flow

Finally as you step into the center of the circle and move to the center of your life, you will be in the flow of self mastery as indicated in Diagram 3 and you will encounter fewer obstacles. It is here that the edges no longer overlap and loop back. At this stage you understand and transmute your fears and blocks and use faith in the Divine to bypass the fears and blocks associated with mystery and the unknown. Your issues and blocks no longer inhibit your ascension process. This is the ultimate goal in actualizing your destiny.

# CHAPTER 4

## Important Components of the Self

### Highest Self

Your highest self is an extension of your soul, and your soul should reside inside your body. The soul is very intense energy and travels through life and infinity. Your highest self is a spiritual bridge between your earth existence and the Divine. Your highest self is earth related and its purpose is to keep you on your Divine path moment to moment.

When you connect to your highest self and direct your energy, the universe opens up to you. Quiet your brain, listen to your highest self and you will find the truth within. In Chapter 16 we discuss discovering the various parts of yourself and determining if they are working together or in conflict with one another. The driving force behind self mastery is your highest self.

Your highest self can be visualized as residing in a gold ball six inches above your head. Access to this energy center can be gained through meditation and hypnosis. In meditation and in hypnosis you are deeply relaxed. This puts you in a vibrational state that allows you to connect with the information center of your highest self.

Your connection to your highest self as well as your intuition and psychic abilities may be stronger at certain times than at others. As you go through the ascension process and integrate your wisdom and abilities, a detoxification and many shifts will occur. These changes can affect you mentally, emotionally, physically and spiritually.

Anytime you release a block, there will be some form of detoxification that takes place. Symptoms include headaches, gastrointestinal distress, lightheadedness, dizziness, waves of grief, memories of past trauma, past life memories and intense physical and emotional pain in former wounds. You can also experience mystical and psychic phenomena as described in Chapters 14 and 17 as part of this process.

Another symptom of the detoxification process that you might experience is the loss of or inability to connect to your highest self. Although this feels horrible, it is a normal part of the detoxification process. Have faith that this condition is temporary and normally lasts no longer than 12 days. When your highest self does return, it will be even more powerful.

During the intermittent time it is suggested that you relax, eat well, get plenty of rest and water and meditate with an open mind. It is particularly useful to use your imagination to determine what your highest self would recommend in any particular situation. Obviously this is not a good time to make life-changing decisions so stay centered, calm and know that your highest self will return.

The following exercise will help you communicate with your highest self. After going through it, begin to practice making decisions through your highest self. Begin with questions like, "Which route should I take to work to encounter the least traffic?" Start your practice by asking questions that are not of great importance. More and more you'll be able to glean helpful information.

As you begin to rely on the accuracy of the information you receive, you'll find it exciting to see and understand things about yourself and other people. But always use discretion in sharing what you have learned with others. A good way to judge whether or not to share information is to ask your highest self if the information will be helpful for the person to know. If yes, share the information; if no, keep it to yourself.

## The Ego

The ego is something that grows and develops. A baby or young child does not yet have one. Its purpose is to protect your Divine calling but sometimes we have difficulty reading these messages. The ego informs you of what is going on in the earth plane. It primarily has to do with relationships, professional dealings and other human interactions. Often the ego acts in an abrupt, hysterical, autocratic, dictatorial manner about situations. But this is not a negative thing. The ego's sole purpose is to protect the person and make sure the person survives. The ego is never satisfied because it needs to continually communicate and keep us informed.

Make friends with your ego—honor it; listen to it. Let your highest self determine how the information provided by your ego should or should not be utilized.

## Feelings

Feelings have their own energy and can be a function of the ego or they can be a function of any other part of the self. Two primary types of feelings exist: pathologic and healthy. The first are destructive and disturbing feelings that float around and are not connected to anything specific that is happening to you in the moment. These feelings are generated by someone else and projected onto you or they are feelings that have built up over time and have not been dealt with.

Healthy feelings get our attention and give us information about anything and everything. When listened to, the feeling will naturally dissipate. When ignored, a healthy feeling can build up and become pathologic.

Use your feelings to help you know and understand what is going on in your life. Then let your highest self guide you in the proper actions. Continual pathological feelings should be addressed in therapy.

In Chapter 16 we will discuss more parts of yourself and how they interact and whether they are in conflict or working together. For now, understanding the purpose of the highest self, ego and feelings is enough.

***Exercise 1: Communicating with your highest self.*** This exercise will help you discover your highest self.

1. Go to a place where you will not be disturbed.
2. Relax your physical body and consciously let go of stress and replace it with peace and harmony.
3. Notice your thoughts and let go of any negativity and replace it with peace and harmony.
4. Notice your feelings and let go of any negativity and replace it with peace and harmony.
5. Place a bubble of peace around you with the intention, "Only good will come to me and only good will leave from me now."
6. Imagine a white sacred corridor starting to form around you and imagine yourself walking down it.
7. At the end of the corridor is a safe staircase; follow it downstairs until you reach a golden corridor.
8. In this golden corridor there are many doorways; each one is labeled.

9. Find the doorway marked with your name and titled "Highest Self."
10. Go into the space and find a comfortable place to sit down.
11. Relax and begin to notice a presence from a distance coming toward you.
12. Allow the being to come toward you and with your mind's eye pay attention to what you see and what you feel.
13. Communicate with the presence.
14. Perhaps the presence has a gift for you.
15. Ask any questions you have at this time.
16. Give yourself time to explore the energy.
17. Thank the presence.
18. Take the presence back with you if you like.
19. Come out of the room, leaving the door open. Walk down the golden corridor to the stairs; go up the stairs to the white sacred corridor.
20. Return to the present moment.
21. Ground yourself completely by stamping each foot three times or more.
22. Make notes in your journal to document this experience and what you have learned.

Afterward, keep checking with your highest self to engage in a deeper, more spontaneous relationship.

# CHAPTER 5

## *Meditation*

Finding peace and harmony within yourself and living your hopes and dreams are the end results of connecting to your highest self. Meditation is the key to making that happen. Meditation is a deep state of alert relaxation and concentration that allows you to perform at your best and tap into more of your unlimited wisdom and potential.

Meditation produces a vibration and energy at a specific level. It is an ageless human experience that has been used in just about every culture and time period. For the many people who have developed and used it throughout the ages, it has brought them strength, serenity and an increased ability to function and find peace and joy.

The concept of meditation is about living in the moment, being mindful, and getting to know yourself—body, mind and spirit. Meditation helps you slow down and focus your attention. It's fitness for the whole self, toning the mind and relaxing the body. With meditation you can reach your potential by getting in touch with who you are and determining what you want to achieve out of life. Meditation can influence all aspects of your life including career, sports and relationships. It also influences your physical, emotional, spiritual and mental health.

Meditation means different things to different people and the form meditation takes can vary. The specific method you select should be based on your current condition; your resources of time, energy and money; and what you hope to accomplish.

Meditation can improve your health by reducing stress. The benefits of meditation include the promotion of healing, faster recovery from stressful events, reduction of insomnia and enhanced pain management. Meditators often find their minds working more efficiently with an increased ability to concentrate. Meditation is age-reversing and twenty minutes of meditation has the value of three hours of sleep.

The meditative state is similar to the state we experience just before we fall asleep. When brain waves of meditators are measured, they exhibit a mixture of alpha and theta waves, the characteristic brain wave patterns that occur between waking and sleeping.

The brain scans of meditators also reveal better blood flow, better connections between different areas of the brain and physiological changes that indicate profound states of relaxation and stress reduction. That's a key health benefit since long-term stress can be extremely detrimental. Unfortunately we often mistake a stressed state for being normal when stress is present over long periods of time.

More and more the medical profession is realizing and utilizing the mind-body-spirit connection. In 1993 the Office of Alternative Medicine was established and in 1998 Congress elevated it to the National Center for Complementary and Alternative Medicine at the National Institutes of Health (NIH). That year 75 out of 117 medical schools in the United States offered elective courses in complementary and alternative medicine or included topics on complementary and alternative medicine in required courses. And, you may have noticed that many medical centers are developing centers for alternative medicine and offer meditation classes and programs concerning the mind, body and spirit connection.

Perhaps the most exciting benefit to meditation is how it leads you into the adventurous and mystical aspect of living life. This will happen when you listen to your highest self and follow what it tells you. Then wondrous, exciting, powerful connections begin to happen.

Many good books have been written about the history and many techniques of meditation. This book emphasizes the essentials to get you going and you are encouraged to do more reading on your own.

## Keys to a Good Practice of Meditation

- **Space:** Find a quiet space where you will be free from interruptions. Use a comfortable chair that supports your spine and keeps it straight while allowing your feet to be flat on the floor. It may be helpful to have a table in front of you on which you can place something from nature that you connect with, such as a flower, plant, rock, crystal or feather. Candles or mandalas also work particularly well. Use the object to focus your gaze.
- **Body and emotion scan:** Imagine that you can scan your body. Use your mind to scan from the top of your head to your feet. As you scan, observe the condition of your body and look for tension, stress and pain. If you find anything negative, imagine that you release it and replace it with peace and relaxation. This shifts your energy so you are balanced. Scan your emotions and notice if you have negative emotions that you are ready to release. Imagine that you

let them go and replace them with peace and calmness.
- **Breath:** Use your breath in meditation to readjust your state of being to deep relaxation. Watch your breath come in and go out. Breathe deep, taking air in through your nose and into your chest and abdomen. As you inhale, visualize taking in white, healing light and exhale any tension or negative thoughts.
- **Thoughts:** Observe your thoughts. Notice if you have any negativity. If you do, imagine that you can let these negative thoughts go and replace them with something that is more beneficial to you now.
- **Cues:** Pay attention to body sensations you feel during meditation such as feelings of heaviness, tingling or slight pressure somewhere in your body. Recognizing these cues will deepen your state of meditation.
- **Tips:** Remember to breathe. Holding your breath raises anxiety. Avoid falling asleep because you lose the benefit of meditation. Start with short meditation periods, 5 to 10 minutes, and increase your time. Follow a regular schedule to help meditation become a part of your life and ensure that you accomplish your goals as your life evolves.
- **Caution:** If pain, anger or anxiety intensifies, stop your practice and try it again another day.

## Chakras

An important aspect of meditation is the flow of life-force energy through the body. While there are hundreds of places in the body where energy is concentrated, there are a dozen major centers, commonly called chakras, that we focus on while meditating. Chakra is a Sanskrit word meaning "wheel" and these centers are similar to wheels in that they are spinning vortices of energy.

Chakras are sometimes referred to as the psycho-spiritual energy centers. The chakras are the mechanism by which the body, mind and spirit integrate as one holistic system. The major chakras are located along the spinal column from the base of the spine to the crown of the head as indicated in Diagram 4.

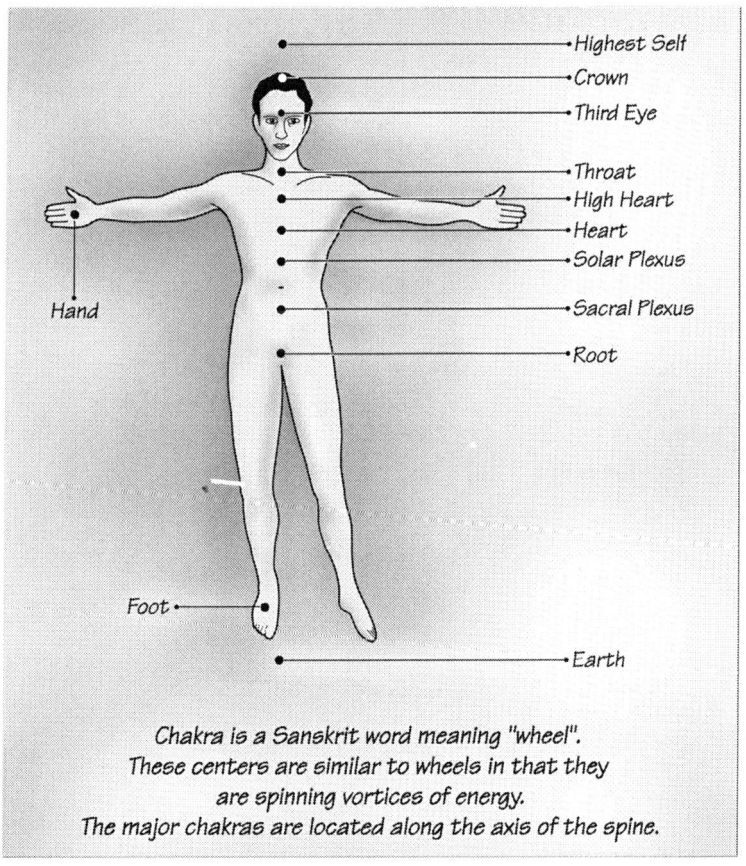

Chakra is a Sanskrit word meaning "wheel".
These centers are similar to wheels in that they are spinning vortices of energy.
The major chakras are located along the axis of the spine.

4 – Body Chakras

These major chakras are associated with specific organs and may be best visualized by specific colors. Each has a significant meaning attached to it. Other important chakras are in the palms of the hands, wrists and at the bottoms of the feet. The earth chakra is located six inches below the feet and the highest self chakra is located above the crown chakra on top of the head. Diagram 5 illustrates these attributes.

| Chakra | Color | Location | Meaning |
| --- | --- | --- | --- |
| Earth Chakra | Red, White, and Gold | Six inches below the feet | Earth foundation |
| Root Chakra | Red | Base of spine and opens downward between the legs | Earth plane, survival, prosperity, relationships |
| Sacral Plexus Chakra | Orange | Lower abdomen connected to the spine; opens to front and back of the body | Creativity, inner child |
| Solar Plexus Chakra | Yellow | Above navel connected to the spine; opens to front and back of the body | Divine will |
| Heart Chakra | Green | Middle of the chest connected to the spine; opens to front and back of the body | Unconditional love, ego |
| High Heart Chakra | Pink | Above chest connected to the spine; opens to front and back of the body | Divine, unconditional love |

Various attributes are associated with each of the chakras as illustrated in this diagram.

5 – Chakra Chart

| Chakra | Color | Location | Meaning |
| --- | --- | --- | --- |
| Throat Chakra | Sky blue | Base of throat connected to the spine; opens to front and back of the body | Intuition; inner, outer and psychic communication |
| Third Eye Chakra | Navy blue | On forehead, above the spot between eyebrows; opens to front and back of the body | Connection to universal truth |
| Crown Chakra | Purple and white | Top of the head | Connects earth and the Divine |
| Highest Self Chakra | Gold, pearlessence | Six inches above the head | All-knowing about callings, individual true callings and purpose |
| Hand Chakra | Green and blue, and spectrum of colors | Center of palms and wrist | Healing |
| Feet Chakra | Green and blue, and spectrum of colors | Center of feet | Healing |

Various attributes are associated with each of the chakras as illustrated in this diagram.

### 5 – Chakra Chart

Chakras can become blocked for various reasons and this prohibits the smooth flow of energy through the body. It is possible to measure chakras for the flow of energy using the pendulum as described in Chapter 9.

## Energy

Divine universal energy refers to white light and solar energy coming from the sky and flowing through the body. This energy is also referred to as Divine white light, chi, ki, qi, prana and other names. When meditating, visualize a silk cord coming from the sky and connecting to the top of your head at your crown chakra. Visualize a channel of white light flowing into your crown chakra.

Earth energy refers to all the energy located around and in the center of the earth. Also picture silk cords coming from your feet, tailbone and the palms of your hands and that these cords connect to the red center of the earth. Draw positive energy from the middle of the earth to increase your feelings of stability, balance, harmony and being grounded.

You can also safely dispose of negative energy using this method. Negativity is anything that interferes with the achievement of your highest goals and values. Dispose of it by imagining it running down the silk cords and returning to the center of the earth to be reprocessed for the good of all.

## Sekhem-Seichim-Reiki

Sekhem-Seichim-Reiki is the integration of three related but distinct energy healing systems. Sekhem-Seichim is from Egypt; Reiki is from Japan. These energy systems work together to harmonize the physical, emotional, mental and spiritual bodies. The high frequency, vibratory light and sound energies help activate healing resources.

Many volumes have been written about these systems and while they are very complementary to the techniques and practices discussed in the book, the scope of this book doesn't allow elaboration on them. They are mentioned here and throughout the book as another resource worth investigating. It is extremely beneficial to obtain training to become a Reiki Master Teacher and a Sekhem-Seichim Master Teacher.

## The Meditation Process

There are many ways to meditate. The following is a simple overview of the process for effectively meditating:

1. Slow down, focus your attention and relax.
2. Imagine you bring up earth energy through your body focusing on the chakras.
3. Imagine you bring in white light from sky energy and mix the earth and sky energy throughout your body.
4. Imagine you wrap a bubble of peace around you and make positive affirmations.

Now, let's study the process in more detail. As suggested earlier, sit in a chair where you will be free from interruption. Make sure your back is straight and your feet are flat on the floor. Starting at the top of your head, scan your body and then your emotions to release any tension or discomfort. As you breathe, imagine you inhale peace and harmony and exhale any negativity.

Imagine that as you breathe in, you draw the energy from the center of the earth up into your feet. Feel warm, relaxing red energy come into your feet, ankles, legs and move up into your chakras. Visualize this energy ascending through your body and encountering each chakra one at a time. Imagine each whirling, spinning chakra mingling with the earth energy and turning its designated color as indicated in the chart. Also think of the color and meaning of each chakra and its relevance to your life at this point in time. The main purpose in working with and understanding the chakras is to create integration and wholeness within you.

Now imagine sky energy is pouring into your crown chakra. See this loving, healing white light flow into you. Feel the perfect amount of energy pour down into each cell, starting at the top of your head and working its way through your whole body six inches below your feet. Then take it back in and up around your body and in through the top of your head creating a continuous flow of energy.

Feel the sky and earth energy boost your self-esteem and inner strength. Picture the earth energy and sky energy mixing, blending and integrating within your body for your maximum health and well being.

Scan your body as indicated earlier in this chapter and shift your energy so that you are balanced. Imagine that there is a giant mirror across from you and visualize glowing, spinning chakras.

Look into the mirror and see yourself as perfectly balanced, feeling great peace and harmony and ready to take on life with new freshness and hope. Now that you are balanced, picture an aura of energy about three feet out around you and filled with white, gold and silver light. Imagine the warm glow you feel runs through the energy in your aura. Imagine that you can completely surround your entire aura with a bubble of peace so that only good can come to you and only good will leave from you. Feel the strength and confidence that this vibration provides.

This meditation does four things:

1. It creates balance.
2. It provides harmony and improved performance by centering and grounding you, increasing energy and creating peace.
3. It connects you to the source of abundance.
4. It provides balance and harmony to the physical body, mental body, emotional body and spiritual body.

As you use this meditation on a regular basis, your sense of balance, stability and confidence will increase for the better. For best results meditate daily. Start with 5-to 10-minute blocks and gradually add time to each session until you are comfortable meditating 20 minutes to an hour each time. Also meditating as part of a class or in a group reinforces the likelihood that you will do it and continue doing it.

## Other Meditations

There are many other types of meditation and you might want to try these at some future time. As indicated previously, sit in a comfortable place with no distractions.

- **Contemplation**—Contemplation is a meditation on something outside of you. Hold an object at a comfortable distance and study it. It's best to start with a natural object like a feather, seashell or stone. The idea is to look at it actively and dramatically but without words. Try to bring yourself to do just one thing and that is to look. The goal is to be totally involved in this intense, non-verbal activity. Suspend your senses and imagination and simply focus your mind on the object. Using the same object every time you meditate can make the exercise go easier. Try it daily for a couple weeks, 10 minutes at a time. After that increase your time to 15 minutes and work up to 20. Expect the results to be different each time.
- **Breath counting**—Counting your breath is a meditation designed to teach and practice the ability to do one thing at a time. This is harder than it sounds but if you practice it consistently, you can obtain positive physiological and psychological benefits. Count your breaths from one to four as your breathe out. Count "one" for the first breath, "two" for the second, "three" for

the third and "four" for the fourth. Then start over again. Do this for 15 minutes. Do not let any thoughts come into your head. If they do, recognize them and let them go. Concentrate only on counting your breaths. Counting 1-4 allows you to keep track without having to focus on what number you are on.
- **Unstructured**—Choose a topic, relationship, question or something you want to ponder.
- **Taped meditations**—There are many meditation tapes available that will guide you through different types of meditations. They can be fun and useful to take you different places.
- **Moving meditations**—Yoga, Tai Chi, QiGong—These can be a good alternative to a sitting meditation when you don't quite feel like sitting still. The three are ancient systems of mind-body maintenance movements. They all involve the flow of energy through body movements. Classes or videotapes are available to teach you how to do it.

Try different forms of meditation for variety and to find the methods most useful to achieve the results you want.

## Physical Changes

When you begin to meditate, your physical, mental, emotional and spiritual functioning will begin to change. As this happens your vibrations will change and so will people and animals around you. As these changes take place, toxins will leave your body. Detoxification is discussed in Chapter 4 as something that occurs as part of the ascension process and may cause your highest self and psychic abilities to shut down temporarily.

Be sure to drink plenty of water and eat fresh foods. Organic foods increase vibrations. Meat, dairy products, caffeine and alcohol can slow the opening of the chakras, so time your meals accordingly. Take good care of yourself and get the rest you need for renewal.

## Grounding

One of the side effects experienced when going through this process is that of feeling detached, spatially challenged, unfocused or confused. If you experience these or similar feelings, it is important to ground yourself. Your aura is a bubble of energy which surrounds you. Grounding is achieved by stating your intention to be in the present and calling back your energy from the past and future.

The concept of grounding actually means being connected to the ground. Things you can do to ground yourself include:

- Imagine that you draw energy from the middle of the earth to increase your feelings of stability, balance and harmony. Have your feet flat on the floor when you do this.
- Eat on a regular basis. Dairy products and meat are very grounding. A high vibrational diet consists of organic fruits and vegetables.
- Use the stone hematite. You can hold it, carry it or wear it.
- Wear man-made fibers as this will slow down the chakra-energy interaction with other people.
- Stomp each foot three times.

## Zen and Living in the Moment

Zen is the beautiful art of accepting each and every thing about life as it is and knowing that everything happening is of the Divine plan. It's the realization that whatever is happening has a deep meaning to you and the essence of your life. Staying calm allows you to be productive in each moment of your life.

Accepting things and being in the moment, however, does not mean you don't need to plan for the future. Being proactive prevents and avoids some of life's pitfalls. Acceptance means striving to be everything you can at any given moment or in any situation. Learn from it and move on.

The concept of meditation is learning to pay attention and live in the moment. It's taking time to smell the roses. Paying attention to the nuances and details of your life is called "meditation while living" or mindfulness. Living in the moment is easier said than done since our lives are generally consumed with so many activities we continually think ahead and live in the future. Or worse, we live in the past and think about what we should have said or done concerning a past activity we cannot change.

Mindful living means being aware of your body, feelings and thoughts, and mind states. It is also understanding that what you think influences the way you act and feel as was discussed in the earlier section on beliefs. It is good to live in the here and now and invest yourself in being totally present in each moment. Give all your energy and attention to your life force one moment at a time.

True power is in mindful living in the here and the now. If you spend too much time thinking in the past or future, it increases anxiety. Reteach yourself to accept everything about your life. An understanding will then come to you about which things you should change and enhance.

For example, a meditation student began exploring her

chakras and found that her root chakra was almost totally closed. She meditated on this and found that as a child she had been very frightened when her family had financial difficulties. As a result of this fear, she unknowingly shut down the energies in her root chakra.

Through this discovery and using the meditation exercises in class, she was able to open her root chakra and deal with her fears of financial instability by being more proactive with her money. This led to an increase of energies in her emotional, mental, physical and spiritual functioning. She took a class in budgeting and investing money. As she attuned to the nature of her financial life, it grew in abundance.

As you explore your own chakras, associate with the meanings and conditions you find there. The awareness will help you make adjustments for better balance and harmony in your life.

The meditation vibration keeps you tapped into the unlimited vital life force of the universe. This is the unlimited source of all prosperity in love, health, relationships, money, time and everything. If you are on your path, listening to your highest self and tapping into the Divine source, you have the mechanism for success firmly in your life.

Through meditation you can connect to the part of yourself that made the original contract with the Divine to appear and live here on the earth plane. The most important things are the motivation and intention that go with each action.

## Keys to Success with Meditation

1. Meditate every day.
2. Meditate at the same time every day because it builds a habit.
3. Meditate in the same space every day.
4. Scan your body, mind and soul for anything negative that

needs to be released and let it go into the middle of the earth where it will be reprocessed for the good of all.
5. Begin by grounding yourself to the earth plane. Bring the earth's energy up through your feet, legs and into each chakra.
6. Connect yourself to the sky energy. Bring the sky energy down into the top of your head and through your body six inches below your feet. Then take it back in and up around your body and in through the top of your head creating a continuous flow of energy.
7. Mentally integrate the earth and sky energy throughout your body.
8. Reinforce the intention of a bubble of peace around you and make the affirmation "Only good will come to me and only good will leave from me now." Imagine a column of white light with the column connecting to the earth and the Divine source.
9. Keep a log of your thoughts, feelings and intuitive insights.
10. Meditation amplifies feelings. So if you are ill, angry or in a bad mood, meditate only lightly or not at all.

***Exercise 2: Meditation.*** In your daily meditation, scan each one of your chakras and explore what is being held in each of these energy spheres. Do whatever work is necessary to purify and enhance the energy. Enter the information in your meditation journal as suggested in Chapter 8.

# CHAPTER 6

## *Empower Your Work with Ethics*

Using high ethical standards is one of the most important things you can do to strengthen and empower your work. Invisible, supernatural forces are real and do exist. They can become more evident when we are connected to our Divine purposes on earth or while we are going through the processes to achieve our goals. This format drives co-creation where you listen to your highest self and follow through on the guidance suggested. This brings the Divine to earth and into your life and moves you toward living your hopes and dreams.

There is an etiquette and ethical standard that should be applied when working with the supernatural. Unfortunately, some people do not practice ethics as they should. They do themselves and everyone else a disservice, creating negativity that will come back to the offending person.

The whole point of ethics is to use a code of conduct guided and directed by the Divine Source to achieve our purpose and callings here on earth now. Using the highest ethics allows you to be the master of your destiny and create synchronicity where the earth plane and supernatural forces come together to make opportunities.

The following are the most important ethical guidelines to use in your metaphysical practices:

1. **Ask permission**—You must always have permission to work with another person by verbally asking, "May I help you with (your situation)?" If you send something positive to another person they didn't ask for or want, they have to receive it. It then piles more onto what they have to do and creates more karma for you. Never assume a person wants your help unless you check with that individual.

    If someone is comatose or not available, you can telepathically ask that person's highest self for permission. If you are not given permission verbally or telepathically to work with a person, you can always pray for the best possible Divine result. You will be greatly rewarded for trusting that there is a Divine order in the universe and everything is happening as it should to teach us the lessons we need to learn.

2. **Control your feelings when using supernatural forces**—Only send positive energy. Be careful if you are struggling with jealousy, resentment, hostility or other negative feelings toward another person. If you inadvertently project anything but the best of intentions, it will come back to you multifold.

3. **Respect the confidential nature of issues**—Always respect the other's privacy; do not repeat what you have heard or tell with whom you have worked. Be discreet with your own metaphysical workings, writings or accessories—particularly around people who might not understand or be supportive. Also, be respectful of other people in the field; they all have something to contribute even if you don't agree with their philosophy.

4. **Know your intention**—Your intention and the motivation behind what you do are the most important parts of

your activities and may be more important than your actual actions. A record exists in the universe of everything that has been said, felt or done and the intention behind the actions. This is called the Akashic Record. An example of the importance of intention versus action is that if a man steals bread to feed his family and intends to repay the baker when he has money, it is very different than the man who steals because he is too lazy to work.

5. **Honor free choice**—Free choice is available to everyone but should not be taken for granted. Never interfere with the free choice of others and always preface your work with the statement, "According to the Divine plan." Remember that free choice can always influence the outcome. Respect and honor free choice for yourself and others moment to moment.

6. **Practice abundance**—Tap into the channel of abundance for yourself and cooperate with others tapping into it for themselves. When you are on your path, abundance is readily available. First tap into your own channel to the Divine Source and then to the channel of abundance. Pain, suffering and feelings of negative self-worth can be barriers to achieving abundance and must be eliminated. The good in pain and suffering is that it can help identify the areas that need work and should be viewed as a gift to be utilized.

7. **Fulfill your destiny**—Each person came to the earth with a purpose of transforming his or her energy and the energy here on earth to that of more love.

8. **Utilize spirit guides**—The realm of spirit guides includes angel, fairy, and goddess; ancestral spirits; animal totems; and spiritual energies attached to disciplines such as Reiki, Sekhem-Seichim, psychology, and so on. These are helpers of the Divine Source and are energies that vibrate peace and harmony. These energies become more pronounced as you become more aware of them and receive guidance

from them. In developing a relationship with the spirit guides, you will be able to ask for help. You should only do this through the guidance of your highest self. Sometimes you may experience the spirits inside or outside of you. Be sure to listen to your highest self as an additional source of information without getting superstitious or idolizing false gods. Spirit guides will help you but they will not tell you what to do. The information connects with your highest self and your highest self helps you communicate with spirits and spirit guides. Work with only the Divine spirits and if you have any doubts about what the spirits are, ask three times "Are you of the Divine?" and ask three more times "Are you of the Divine purpose?" If they are not of the Divine, they will vanish.
9. **Understand the Law of Karma**—What you send out, you get back. Karma is about unpaid debts or something that is owed to you. You have to clear these blocks to function optimally. If something is happening in your life that you do not want to happen, ask what it is trying to teach you and where it comes from. This way you can pay off the karmic debts through understanding and right action so you can transform the situation.
10. **Practice humanistic values**—These are the attitudes that facilitate our abilities to empower and unite with ourselves. Honor these principles:

    - Cooperation as opposed to competition—With the law of abundance, we can all succeed and achieve our goals.
    - Freedom with responsibility—We have the ultimate freedom to do what we want but there is a responsibility that goes along with it.
    - Authenticity—This is about our own truth. Be comfortable with your truth, thoughts and how you feel about things.

- Being in the here and now—That is where our power is—to be proactive and immediate moment to moment.

11. **Accept and project love**—Accept everything that happens moment to moment as the Divine. Be proactive by transforming feelings into unconditional acceptance and love.

Some examples of asking permission include:

- A woman had a dog that chewed on the furniture. She telepathically asked the dog's highest self for permission to speak to it. Using a pendulum, the woman asked the dog's rationale behind the behavior. She found the dog was bored; she asked what could be done. The dog communicated the needs to be walked more often and to receive more attention. The woman agreed and the dog's behavior changed immediately.
- A woman's sister-in-law was being unkind to her. She asked to speak to the woman's highest self and was told "NO." The woman prayed for the best possible outcome according to the Divine plan. Once she prayed, the woman found the friction and tension between herself and her sister-in-law were greatly reduced even though she never actually communicated with the woman's highest self.

***Exercise 2: Obtaining telepathic permission.*** Imagine a person with whom you wish to work. Contact the individual telepathically to ask permission to work with his or her highest

self. In order to obtain telepathic permission, you can do the following sequence:
1. Imagine a pyramid with the top cut off.
2. In meditation, imagine that your highest self invites the highest self of the other person to the top of the pyramid.
3. If the person's highest self and your highest self agree, then you have telepathic permission to work with the person. If not, pray for the best possible outcome according to the Divine plan.

# PART II

# Tools and Techniques
# to
# Enhance Your Experiences

# CHAPTER 7

## *Mind Mapping*

After meditating regularly for a few days, you probably noticed that your thoughts are clearer and you have many new ideas. One effective way to quickly capture these is to use a technique called mind mapping. People use it in different ways. Writers use it to generate ideas for projects or stories they are writing. Businesses use it to collect and communicate ideas. Leonardo daVinci and other great minds of all time have used this technique and you can use it too.

Use mind mapping in conjunction with meditation because meditation sparks mental activity. Mind mapping helps you get ideas down on paper. If you let the mind go freely, it can be very creative. However, when listing ideas in a linear form, people often become stifled trying to determine where to start or what goes where. Negative thinking can also trap them or they let their inner critics take over and encourage them to give up.

Mind mapping is a creative experience that allows you to use your mind and brain cooperatively to chart ideas. Although it is a simple activity, it is very powerful because it goes in a circular, never-ending pattern and groups things together, just like the brain does. Diagram 6 illustrates a mind map outline for an instructional tape on meditation.

Use the following process to do a mind map.

1. Start with the title of the idea you want to develop.
2. Take a big sheet of plain paper and write the idea in the center.
3. Place a circle around the title.
4. Begin meditating and for each idea that surfaces, draw a line out from the circle and write the idea on top of the line. Use different colors of pens to indicate different idea groupings. Use words and drawings to communicate your thoughts.
5. Go back to each idea and see what else comes to mind and add lines off those ideas. You will quickly notice that if you take the time, you can go on for a very long time with all these things you know and think about.
6. After you are done writing all of your ideas, clump information that goes together into themes and related subjects.
7. Have fun accessing your brain and mind for ideas and information.

***Exercise 3: Mind map.*** Meditate on the idea of self-mastery and what it means to you. Then make up a mind map to capture your ideas.

*Self Mastery*

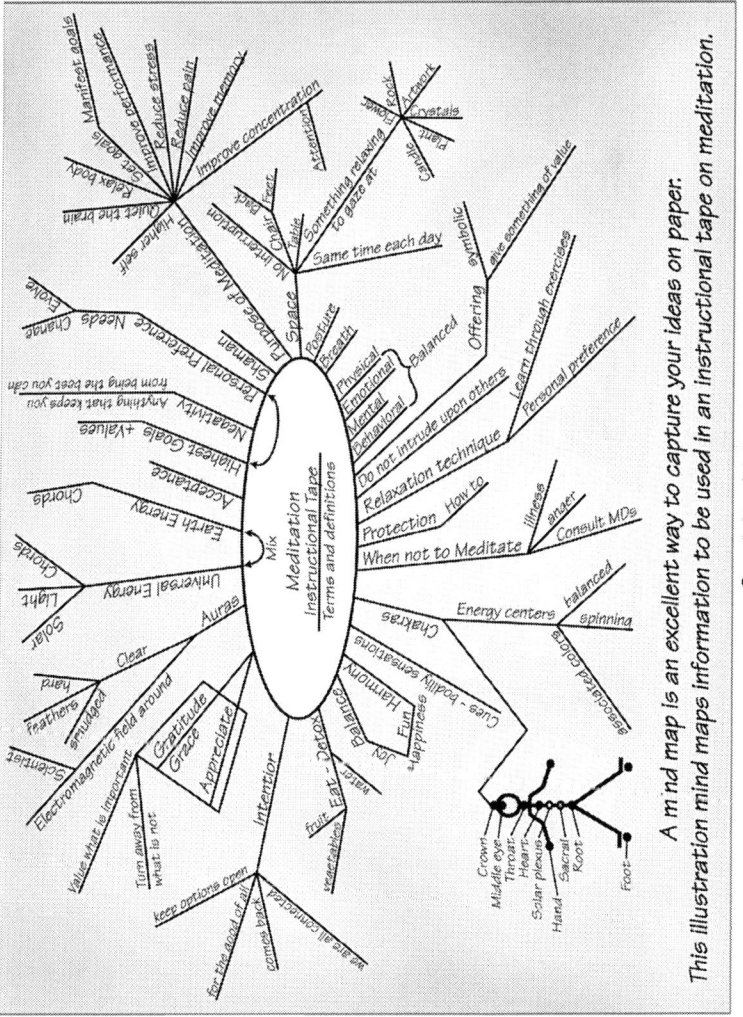

6 – Mind Map

A mind map is an excellent way to capture your ideas on paper.
This illustration mind maps information to be used in an instructional tape on meditation.

# CHAPTER 8

## *Journaling*

While mind mapping is an excellent way to capture the multitude of ideas generated in meditation, journaling helps make and track changes in your life. You've probably tried to make changes in the past with varying degrees of success. One reason resolutions fail is that change and the good things in life do not come without effort. You have to work for them. You can't just resolve to do something and have it happen. You need to develop a plan of action with steps for follow through if you want to change.

Keeping a journal is an excellent way to create, maintain and complete desired goals and changes. Journaling helps you get in touch with yourself and identify what is going on in your life. It is the ultimate tool in co-creating because it helps you follow through with the guidance and actions suggested to you by your highest self.

The act of putting words on paper can make resolutions become more meaningful and real. A journal serves as a chronological document of where you are day to day. Journals can turn into teaching guides and powerful quick references for growth. They are helpful because it's difficult to see the process of growth while you are within it. When you review a journal and see where you started, you often find an amazing transformation taking place. So it is an excellent way to see and monitor your progress and success.

## Types of Journals

There are several different types of journals. The following is a list of kinds of journals that can be used to make changes in your life. For best results, create a journal that encompasses several of the following as sections within it.

- ♦ ***Resolutions/goal journal***—This is your strategic plan. Enter the date, what your goal is and what you want to accomplish. Determine what your next steps are to reach your goal. Refer to this section regularly to monitor your progress and continually determine the next step to reach your goal. This type of journal is a powerful way to make progress, recognize growth and propel you to more success.
- ♦ ***Meditation journal***—Track ideas that occur to you in meditation and use it to monitor your hopes and wishes. You can also use meditation to help you set goals and follow through on them.
- ♦ ***Gratitude journal***—List the things you appreciate and for which you are grateful. Make an entry every day. The best thing about this journal is that the things you pay attention to in your life are the things that grow and develop.
- ♦ ***Night dream journal***—Track your nighttime dreams. This is an excellent tool to get in touch with your inner self since dreams are made of the things in our subconscious. This also puts you in touch with your creative, intuitive self.

Keep the journal by the nightstand to immediately document your dreams upon waking. This is important since dreams can be quickly forgotten. If you don't normally remember dreams, this process may be helpful in stimulating your recall. You may also gain insight into yourself and have fun by interpreting your dreams and the significance of their meanings.

## Tips to Keep in Mind

- ***Purchase a special notebook***—The act of purchasing a special notebook to use as your journal is a powerful affirmation of your commitment. If you're creating your journal on the computer, you may want to print your pages and insert them into a notebook since this will be a quick and easy reference.
- ***Work with a coach or a friend on this project***—The act of simply sharing the information with another person can make you more committed to achieving positive results. Set a weekly meeting to review your progress with one another. The idea is similar to doing physical exercise with a coach or friend; having someone share the activity makes it more fun and strengthens your commitment. This type of journal is a powerful way to make progress, recognize growth and propel you to more success.
- ***Include meaningful items***—Your journal can contain more than just your words—you may want to staple, tape or paste special items into it.
- ***Use positive affirmations***—Positive self-talk is very helpful. Write a positive affirmation in

your journal each day. The affirmation goes right to the unconscious mind and can be activated in your everyday life. More information on affirmations is included in Chapter 12.
- ***Use discretion***—The information you enter in your journal is private. The contents should not be read by others without your permission. If confidentiality of very private information cannot be protected, perhaps it is best to not enter it.

Journaling is a very powerful technique to uncover and work with the conscious, unconscious and outside forces that motivate us. Over time you can see tremendous growth and improvement, particularly if you make journaling a part of your life and can look back on weeks, months and even years of work.

***Exercise 4A: Develop a meditation journal.*** Develop a meditation journal to track the ideas that come to you during or after meditation.

1. Determine how you will keep your notes. Will you write in a notebook, journal or use the computer?
2. Make a journal entry with the date and ideas that come to you each time you meditate.
3. Review the journal weekly to see if these ideas fall into any categories or if you see any patterns developing. This is also a good time to check to see if you have done anything about items that required action.
4. Review the journal monthly to see if a big picture is developing. Should a section of this journal become a goals journal? Perhaps this would be a good time to develop a mind map using the ideas generated.
5. Review the journal periodically to see the growth that has

taken place in your life.

***Exercise 4B: Develop a dream journal.*** Track your nighttime dreams in a journal for two weeks. Keep the journal by your bedside so that you can enter information in it as soon as you wake up. If you don't normally remember your dreams, the act of doing this may be helpful in stimulating your recall. After two weeks review the journal. What do you see emerging? Are there any patterns or themes? What do you think this means?

# CHAPTER 9

## *Pendulum Power*

The pendulum is another method to learn more about your intuition and to utilize the meditative process to access universal truth. This is a powerful tool and will help you achieve more of what you want in your lifetime. A pendulum is not good at fortune telling because free will and minute-to-minute changes affect the outcome of events. It will, however, give you information on the strongest present position for outcomes at this moment.

A pendulum can be used to communicate with the highest self. The use of the pendulum stems from the use of a dowsing rod. Dowsing rods are used to locate water, gold or objects in the ground or sea.

The art goes back to ancient times. Ancient shamanic people were highly sensitive to changes in their environment. They relied completely on their own powers of observation and sensitivity and on those of the animals, which they studied in great detail. They knew that everything had a distinctive energy field associated with it. Their methods of finding and reading these fields have come down to us as dowsing.

Dowsing is the use of a simple tool that emphasizes special small movements in the hand. These movements occur automatically as the body senses the subtle energies emitted by everything around. The more you practice, the better you will become.

The pendulum works by connecting to the highest self while you are in a relaxed state of mind. The information is registered on the brain and passed down through the arm to the hand by the nerves in the nervous system. If you are emotional about a subject, it may be difficult to be objective enough to get an accurate reading.

## How to Use the Pendulum

A pendulum is like any other tool you use; you need to develop a relationship with it and practice to perfect your technique. To use the pendulum, communicate telepathically to ask if you have permission to work with it. If you have permission, ask the pendulum if it needs to be cleared. If so, clear it through your intention and ask the inappropriate energy to leave. Replace the energy that's left with white light. You are now ready to work with the pendulum and can follow these steps:

1. Hold a pendulum and teach it to answer "Yes" by showing it to swing back and forth in front of you, vertically. Teach it to answer "No" by showing it the horizontal motion in front of you. Show it how to go around in a circle, clockwise, which will represent the answer, "Ask another question." Do not hold the pendulum directly over your body or metal objects because they have an electrical charge. There are different ways to hold it. Some people hold it closer to themselves, others farther away. Try a couple different positions to figure out what works for you.
2. Go into a meditative state of mind and body. Think of your issue or question.

3. Ask for the highest of all Divine assistance.
4. Ethics is an important issue as already discussed. You don't want to ask nosey questions. Nor should you interfere with free will. Ask the pendulum three questions:

    ♦ May I ask this question? (You are asking for Divine permission.)
    ♦ Should I ask this question? (You are asking if it is in your best interest and that of others to pursue this question.)
    ♦ Can I ask this question? (You are asking if you have enough skill to utilize the answer for the highest good of all.)

Once you have answers to the above questions, proceed asking specific questions.

1. Ask your question and wait until the pendulum swings automatically.
2. Keep the pendulum protected. Preserve your energy on it. Separate it from other pendulums and don't let other people touch or use them.
3. There are hundreds of applications for the use of the pendulum. However, follow all the rules of ethics including:

    ♦ Don't ask intrusive questions or questions you would not ask a person to his or her face.
    ♦ Always ask for permission from another person's highest self before working with him or her, present or otherwise.
    ♦ If you ask about future events, remember that free will can always change what looks possible or inevitable right now.

## Measuring Chakras

Another use of the pendulum is to measure chakras and the flow of energy. Hold the pendulum about 6 inches in front of the chakra and ask it to show you how much it is open. If the chakra is open, the pendulum will move in a circular direction clockwise or counterclockwise. If you measure the chakras on another person, always ask permission.

You can open chakras by putting your left hand six inches above your head and the right hand in front of the chakra. Move your hand in front of the chakra in a circular, clockwise motion. If doing this on someone else, put your left hand above their head and your right hand in back of their chakra.

Start at the root chakra at the base of the spine and work your way up. Imagine the color of the chakra and that it is spinning and opening. This is an excellent way to obtain more energy. When you're done, hold both hands above the crown chakra. Make sure to release energy by putting your hands under cold running water.

***Exercise 5: Practice using the pendulum with an apple.*** Practice using a pendulum by doing the following exercise with an apple. Apples hold charges and are good training tools for the pendulum. Communicate telepathically to ask the pendulum for permission to work with it. If granted permission, ask if it needs to be cleared. If so, clear it through your intention and ask the inappropriate energy to leave. Replace it with white light. You are now ready to work with the pendulum and can follow these steps:

1. Hold a pendulum and teach it to answer you "Yes" by showing it to swing back and forth in front of you, vertically. Teach it to answer "No" by showing it the horizontal motion in front of you. Show it how to go around in a clockwise circle, which will represent the answer, "Ask

another question." Remember to avoid holding the pendulum directly over your body or metal objects. Try different ways of holding the pendulum until you find what works for you.
2. Place an apple on a table in front of you. Ask the apple for permission to speak to it:

- May I ask this question?
- Should I ask this question?
- Can I ask this question?

Now ask the apple, "Do you have a positive or negative charge?" Tell the pendulum to show you a positive charge by swinging in a vertical fashion and a negative charge by swinging in a horizontal fashion. Measure the charge in the apple. (Most often the top of the apple contains a positive charge and the bottom contains a negative charge.) Measure the charge in your left and right hands. (Most often the left hand has a negative charge and the right hand has a positive charge.) Measure the charge in your left and right knees. (Most often the left knee has a negative charge and the right knee has a positive charge.) When you're finished, place your hands under cold running water to release excess energy.

# CHAPTER 10

## *Aura Viewing*

The energy field that surrounds each person is called the aura. This energy is measurable and detectable. It has been scientifically identified and photographed. A healthy person has an aura that extends out around the body somewhat like an egg shape.

The energy that makes up the aura is a vital life force that has been filtered through an individual's mental, physical, emotional and spiritual energy channels. The energy around a person's body can be seen in shapes, colors, spirit guides, animals, etc. Each person's psychic abilities allow for unique and diverse perceptions of auras. No one sees an aura in exactly the same way.

The aura is a reflection of a person's mental, emotional, physical and spiritual condition. Viewing an aura is helpful because it helps you see spirit guides, past life issues and imbalances. Generally, images viewed on the person's left have to do with the past, while images on the person's right and in front have to do with the future. In addition, images in front of the body are of the earth, and the back of the body are of the spiritual.

If you are shown information when viewing an aura, ask

your highest self what you are to do with the information to help yourself or another.

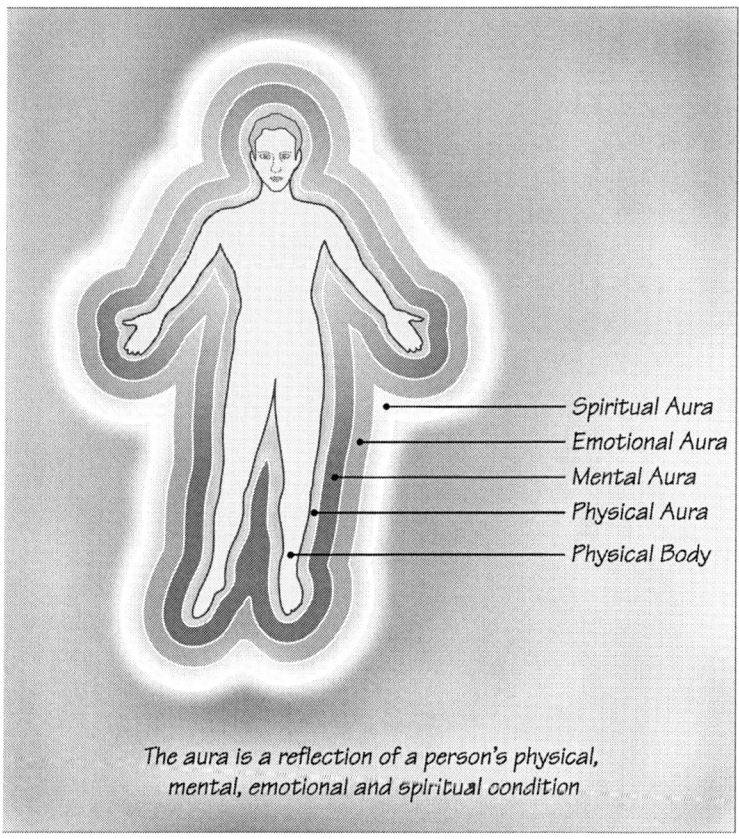

The aura is a reflection of a person's physical, mental, emotional and spiritual condition

7 – Aura

The stronger and more vibrant the aura is, the healthier and the less likely a person is to be influenced by outside forces. Renew and refresh the aura by refraining from the behaviors that weaken the aura. The aura is weakened by poor diet, lack of exercise, lack of fresh air, lack of rest, stress, alcohol, drugs, tobacco, negative habits and improper psychic activity. Participate in activities to refresh and renew the aura through daily exercise, eating a healthy diet of fresh foods, and by doing as the American Indian does—smudging the aura with smoke from sage and cedar.

One of the values of meditation is the grounding and centering effect that it has on the auric field. When in a balanced state, the auric field radiates around the body about three feet. Introverted, withdrawn people hold their aura close to their physical bodies. Hyperactive and unfocused people scatter their auras around them.

Some people see auras, others feel or sense them. When you view a person's aura, you're more likely to be able to do psychic readings. You may also find a knack for doing medical intuitive work or psychic intuitive work. When you become aware of and can interpret auras, you may want to use what you see to help a person understand what is going on within them medically, emotionally and spiritually. Become more aware of auras and more adept at perceiving them through practice.

***Exercise 6: Aura viewing.*** Use the following process to help you view auras. Remember to ask for permission to view a person's aura.

1. Stare into the flame of a candle for at least one minute. Close your eyes and move your earth eyes up to the middle eye in your forehead and view the after-image.
2. Stare at the candle for at least one minute and then look at a blank wall or sheet of paper.
3. To view a person's aura, stare at the person's forehead for at least one minute. As you do this you will notice that things become hazy and begin to glow and look rather neon. This experience is called psychic viewing. When you have this experience, look to the right of the person and notice the after image and how it changes. Look back at the person's forehead for 20 seconds and look back at

the right and you may see shapes and colors. Ask your highest self what it means. Ask the person if he or she would like to hear what you received.

As you do the above exercise notice what you see around the person. You may see slight colors or even images of guides.

# CHAPTER 11

## *Time*

The metaphysical rule on time is that past, present and future occur simultaneously and the brain sorts it out in a linear way. This way we have a frame of reference with a limit and structure in which we work. Through meditation and affirmations to your unconscious mind, you can alter time.

### Manipulating Time

If you are running late and need more time, use this affirmation: Say out loud, "One minute begins to feel like 10 minutes, now." Repeat this several times. Remain calm and proceed as if you have the time you need. Tap into the universal life force of abundance that will enable you to do the work you came to earth to do. You can also do similar affirmations to tap into universal abundance for money and love.

If you are experiencing a situation that is tedious or not pleasant, use this affirmation to shorten time: Say out loud, "Ten minutes begin to feel like one minute, now." Repeat this several times.

Another good situation for manipulating time is when you

have to attend a challenging or difficult function. You can travel to the future event and plant positive seeds for how things will go. In order to manifest for the future, meditate and travel to the future location and insert the feelings and images you want to occur. Don't forget to include the intention of, "For the highest good of all and Divine purposes only."

Envision a positive scenario of how you might react if certain situations arise. Send positive love to yourself for this future event. When you actually go to the event, recite affirmations to shorten time.

You can also travel to the past using time manipulation and remove or correct anything that has already taught you a lesson that you now own. In meditation, travel back in time to a situation you want to change. Relive the scenario the way in which you would have preferred it to happen. This is a good way to remove past pain and grief and put the situation behind you so that you may go forward.

The affirmations and activities work best if you are in an open, relaxed state so that your unconscious mind will hear your command and bring forth your desires effortlessly and easily.

**Exercise 7: Travel back through time.** Think of an experience you had that did not go the way you wanted and is bothersome to you. Go into a meditative state and travel back to the scene and relive the experience as you would have liked it to happen.

# CHAPTER 12

## *Affirmations and Self-Hypnosis*

### Affirmations

Affirmations are powerful orders that you state to your unconscious mind. When you perform affirmations with confidence, the unconscious mind easily and effortlessly brings you what you should have.

We've all had the experience of wanting to buy a certain item that may not be readily available and then suddenly find several. This is also multiplied once friends are told that we are looking for it. The power of the idea builds and increases and becomes much more tangible as we make hopeful statements that are reinforced by others.

A powerful multi-use affirmation is "Only good is coming to me and only good will leave from me now." When making specific affirmations, leave them open-ended so the universe will bring the best possible experiences and you don't limit yourself. It is always wise to say, "The very best prosperity is coming to me now or the best possible love, career opportunities, family situations" and so on.

Be aware that your unconscious mind can be influenced

negatively by what you or others say. So you don't want to say something like, "I need a break" because it might come true and you could end up with a broken leg!

Similarly, if you say, "I will be poor forever," that is what your mind will bring you. A better affirmation would be, "Peace and prosperity are coming to me now." If you have a difficult relationship that doesn't work, use the affirmation, "The best possible relationship is coming to me now."

For example, a woman wanted a baby but had several miscarriages. For her the best affirmation would be, "The best possible opportunities for me to use my nurturing abilities are coming to me now." Then the universe can bring her the best possible experiences for her to utilize her nurturing energies.

Subliminal influences are those influences of which you are not consciously aware. Most commonly they occur on TV, and within movies, magazines and newspapers but they are also in audio images on the radio and telephone. Beware that other people's opinions influence you in ways that may not be in your best interest. Also we are vulnerable to subliminal influences while sleeping. Your unconscious can hear things on the TV or radio while you are asleep.

As you meditate, you open doors to your unconscious mind. Positive self-talk is so important since the unconscious often brings what you mentally and verbally say to yourself. Think about how you may be currently using self-talk. If the affirmations don't produce the results you desire, check with the parts of yourself as indicated in Chapter 16 to determine where there might be areas of disagreement with your goals.

***Exercise 8: Affirmations.*** Develop powerful affirmations that will bring to you your every dream and wish.

- ♦ Write down a few sayings that you repeat to yourself that are negative.
- ♦ Write the negative effect you think these have

had on you in the past.
- Write what would be more effective and positive self-talk for the way that you want your life to be now.
- Write your affirmations on cards and put these cards in several locations where you will see them often. These would be places like in your wallet, on the dashboard, on the refrigerator, in your desk drawer. Make sure that you place these so that anyone negative to your hopes and dreams will not see them.

## Self-Hypnosis

Hypnosis is a process by which the conscious mind goes to sleep and the unconscious mind becomes available. The unconscious mind knows everything and can actually find desired outcomes and bring them to you, easily and effortlessly. The greatest changes will take place when there is agreement between a person's unconscious and highest self.

The unconscious mind can also heal the body, mind, soul or karma level. This is most powerful when done in conjunction with an individual's highest Divine purposes. All of us have certain issues or lessons we need to learn in order to transform our energy to a higher vibration of unconditional love and acceptance.

When something is removed from the unconscious mind, another thing must replace it. If you cannot think of a better replacement, do not remove it until you do. In other words, if you want to stop a bad habit, you must replace it with a new, more adaptive one. If you do not replace the old behavior with a new one, your entire system could go into chaos.

## Self-Hypnosis Process

Go to a place where you will not be disturbed. Play soft, enjoyable music. Sit in a chair that is comfortable and supports your back. Look up at the ceiling and find a spot on which to focus your eyes. Stare at this spot, without blinking. Your eyelids will become very heavy and want to close. But hold them open until your eyelids become so heavy that you can no longer hold them open.

1. When your eyes close, scan your body, emotions, and mind for any kind of negativity, distress or discomfort that you would like to release into the middle of the earth where it will be reprocessed for the good of all. Replace the negativity with peace, harmony and balance.
2. Bring up earth energy into your entire body through each chakra.
3. Bring in sky energy through the top of your head and down through your body.
4. Wrap a bubble of peace around your aura.
5. Tell your conscious mind to rest and go to sleep.
6. Take each affirmation and state it out loud to your unconscious.
7. Make an image in your mind of already achieving the outcome and experience the feelings that this success gives you now. Emphasize emotions that will help you feel satisfied and secure.
8. After you are done going through each affirmation, make the statement "It is done."
9. Tell your conscious to wake up and integrate your conscious mind, body, unconscious mind and highest self in a perfect way for you now.

Do this exercise regularly.

***Exercise 9: Positive self-affirmation.*** Think of an area of your life that is not going as well as you would like. Design an affirmation to get the desired results. Perform the self-hypnosis process and send the affirmation to your unconscious mind.

Here is a hint: In designing your affirmation, always state, "According to the Divine plan, the best possible _____ is coming to me now, easily and effortlessly. And it is done."

# CHAPTER 13

## *Circles*

The circle symbol has a powerful effect on the mind. Circles can create balance, promote healing and help you go into meditation. Some of the forms circles take are spirals, mandalas, stone circles, the moon, labyrinths and medicine wheels.

Our ancestors believed everything in life is circular with one phase merging into the other and beginning again. We observe the changing of the seasons, the traveling direction of the sun and the moon and how we develop from birth to death. We are one within the circle of life.

## Mandalas

Mandalas are artistic renditions of a circle. They relax the brain and open creativity. Stare at them and they come to life. They are empowering and healing. Mandalas have been used as powerful symbols of universal principles by cultures all over the world. They typically have balance and symmetry and are used for healing and spiritual union.

*Mandalas are used for healing and spiritual union. They typically have balance and symmetry.*

*8 – Mandala*

## Stone circles

Stone circles like Stonehenge are places where the ancients met. Many stone circles remain throughout Britain, Ireland and other parts of the world. There is speculation that some were built as burial sites, though not necessarily for this purpose exclusively. However, many small sites have no evidence of burials. It is thought that the majority of circles was used as meeting places for trading and ceremonial practices, rituals and festivities.

It's also thought that the stone circles may have been used as calendars because their paths are oriented to the sun, moon and larger stars. Many stone circles are built on ley lines (earth magnetic energy lines) and provide some paranormal power.

## The Moon

The moon's cycles were used to keep track of time before calendars were created. The moon has a natural rhythm and its phases have played a crucial role throughout history and continue to the current time.

- Planting of crops—The phases of the moon have played an instrumental role in planting and harvesting crops (called "biodynamic farming" today).
- Tides—The gravitational pull of the moon causes the ocean levels to change from hour to hour and day to day.
- People's behavior—Mental health or hospital emergency room workers agree that they see more erratic behaviors in people at the full moon.
- Holy days—Certain religions track their holy days according to the phases of the moon.

The full moon has been a time of celebration, with many rituals established in alignment with it. The other phases of the moon can be quite powerful, depending on our intentions, and it may be worthwhile to synchronize activities with the lunar rhythms

9 – The Moon

The full moon has been a time to celebrate for thousands of years and many rituals have been established in alignment with it. However the other phases of the moon can be quite powerful depending on our intentions. Overall it may be worthwhile to synchronize activities with the lunar rhythms.

- ♦ New moon: Start things—This is the time for new beginnings. The solar and lunar pulls are in the same direction and it is a good time to

look at our dreams and waking inspirations. Intuition is more accessible.
- ♦ First Quarter: Complete things—This is a time to work on things already begun. It is a good time to produce, complete and add to work.
- ♦ Full moon: Celebrate—The full moon is time for completion and time to put to use what has been worked on. Celebrate and evaluate accomplishments at this powerful time.
- ♦ Last Quarter: Dismantle—This is a time of sorting, clearing and finishing. It is time to streamline and eliminate the unnecessary, to clear out and make room for the new.

## The Labyrinth

The labyrinth is an ancient archetype we see in various forms and religious traditions throughout the world. The design varies from a simple spiral to complicated patterns. Although it appears similar to a maze, a labyrinth will always lead you to the center and have only one path in and out as indicated in Diagram 10.

Labyrinths were used in many civilizations throughout time. Unfortunately by the seventeenth and eighteenth centuries, European labyrinths lost their spiritual meaning and this led to the destruction of some of them. Fortunately some were saved and records of others exist. Today the labyrinth is experiencing a resurgence as a sacred form. Churches are incorporating them into the architecture and landscape. Groups are building them into parks and on private land. Spas are incorporating them into their offerings.

*The design varies from a simple spiral to complicated patterns. Although it appears similar to a maze, a labyrinth will always lead you to the center, and have only one path in and out.*

### 10 – Labyrinth

Walking a labyrinth can make you feel more balanced. It's an excellent metaphor for life and symbolizes our life from birth to death. Its twists and turns can easily represent the confusing and conflicting pathway we travel daily. And just when you are closest to the center, it may appear that you are farthest away. Walking the labyrinth can be a way of deepening your own spiritual journey. Following the pathway can create the balance between the inner and outer worlds and ultimately to our deepest center.

As you enter, ask yourself a question or state your intention. Let this question or intention guide you to the center. The center is a place for meditation and prayer, a place for openness and receiving. Listen for guidance and ask your highest self for interpretation. As people follow the path out from the center, they often experience a sense of wholeness, healing and empowerment.

Return to the outer world with your experience and remember you may have a different experience each time you walk the labyrinth. Many people report experiencing amazing insights and intuition while walking a labyrinth.

## The Medicine Wheel

Medicine wheels are energy sources and are used for healing, teaching and understanding. They are also used for reflecting on life and celebrating joyous occasions. The medicine wheel teaches us balance and to discover our path and selves.

Before the Europeans came to North America, there were about 20,000 medicine wheels developed by Native Americans. Native Americans respected and honored everything. Medicine wheels vary by tribe, although the basic concepts are similar.

Stones make up a medicine wheel and are laid out in a symbolic, circular pattern as indicated in Diagram 11. Each stone has a simple meaning and additional interpretations are possible. The cycles of nature, day and night, seasons, moons, life cycles and orbits of celestial bodies are depicted in the circle.

The directions the stones face have a specific significance. The east is about beginning and birth. The south is about nurturance. The west is about mystery. The north is about wisdom. The center is a direct opening to the Divine Source or cosmic connections.

Made of stones, medicine wheels are energy sources used for healing, teaching and understanding. The stones are laid out in a symbolic, circular pattern.

*11 – Medicine Wheel*

Every project goes through cycles. If you are working on a project you can call on the directions to help you. Other parts of the medicine wheel are the elements: earth, wind, fire, and water. You can call on the elements for help too if you use them with respect.

When creating a medicine wheel, call upon the directions, the moon, the sun, the elements and the spirits to help manifest needs and to remember who we are, what is to come, and why we are here. When finished, dismantle the stones to close the energies.

# PART III

# Advanced Techniques

# CHAPTER 14

## *Mystical Experiences*

If you've been meditating, connecting to your highest self and doing the exercises as suggested, chances are you are experiencing some mystical events in your life. But, just what is a mystical experience? They are experiences of unity and knowing unlike any other. In general you know the event is not a dream, visualization, memory or something you are creating. Typically it manifests as being profoundly real like a regular conversation but with a reality all its own.

There are realms of enchantment that act as havens outside the mundane earth existence. This realm is one of inspiration, intrigue and surprise that empowers and excites your life. It is in this place that knowledge can be gained and lessons learned if you only look around and realize what is happening.

Examples of these occurrences are:

- Memories that are not about this current life time.
- Information received about the future.
- Information received about the past.
- Contact with a person who has left the earth.
- Contact with beings at a sacred site.

- Occurrences while sleeping that are not dreams but occur in another realm.
- Contact with spirit beings such as angels, ascended masters, deities, fairies, and animals.

These experiences can be received through sight, feeling and/or hearing. They may be experienced inside or outside of you. Most likely this mystical experience phenomenon has to do with energy from the goddess, fairy realm, spirit guides, angels or sacred sites. Let's take a closer look at each one of these.

## Goddess Energy

Goddess energy is about love, unity and the interconnectedness of all things. It has a strong spiritual vibration and is based on the principle that we are all one. It also guides intuition. Goddess energy is about abundance of all things including love, relationships, career, success and money. It's about being cooperative rather than competitive. The purpose of the goddess is to make the earth a wonderful place to be.

Although the term goddess is feminine, goddess is neither male nor female but a combination of both. It's a balance of yin and yang, white light, unconditional love and acceptance.

Goddess energy can be inside or outside you. It can be visual, auditory, or a feeling. It has a quality of knowing as opposed to believing and is an unusual experience that doesn't match everyday occurrences.

During recent years the goddess energy has flooded the earth and some amazing things have begun to happen. One is that the veils between the dimensions have begun thinning and more people have become clairvoyant and intuitive. Many people started searching for their own spiritual paths.

Integration of the goddess energy can be euphoric and exciting. It begins with ascension as described in the discussion on self mastery. You begin taking in more white light and vital life force. You spiral up and around and connect to your vision of your hopes and dreams and remember why you came to earth and this is wonderful. However, then you remember why you have not achieved your goals and loop back. You touch your blocks and issues and it is painful.

This can be confusing because you are taking in more white light yet experiencing your worst fears. The best way to handle this is to be grounded, heal your blocks and deal with your issues as previously discussed. It is most important to connect to your faith and trust in the higher power.

Signs of taking in the goddess include:

1. The goddess will connect to your highest self to help you understand your callings and purposes.
2. When the goddess energy is with you, it will defend the truth and your rights in amazing ways. For example, an incident occurs which you consider minor; however, people react very strongly to your power.
3. The goddess is magnetic. You might think about someone and he or she appears or calls.
5. The goddess draws to you the things you should have. Of course the "should haves" are determined by your highest self and your life purpose.
6. You easily manifest your hopes and dreams.
7. You feel centered, grounded and almost euphoric.
8. People may ask you if you are in love.

A key thing about incorporating goddess energy is doing everything with a sense of meaning, purpose and love. It is wise to always consider your motivations and intentions in everything you do.

The goddess can bring many positive things into your life

and is interested in prosperity but not at the exclusion of someone else. If you are a competitive person, practice abundance to find yourself becoming more cooperative. Also, the goddess is interested in building unity among people but demands that everyone pull his or her own weight.

The goddess energy can spontaneously appear or you can invite it in. The energy can be invoked where you experience it inside your head or evoked where you experience it outside of yourself. Access the goddess energy through the following techniques:

- Meditate regularly.
- Use circles; they are very important in goddess practice. Mandalas and medicine wheels are very powerful to meditate on and to practice with. They balance you, ground you, and bring you into harmony.
- Work with vital life force energies such as Reiki-Sekhem-Seichim.
- Pay attention to the goddesses you know about; do research to learn more about them as well as other goddesses you may not be familiar with.
- Invite the goddess in by creating a home altar as discussed in the meditation section. Make a sacred space where you can have pictures or symbols of the goddess. Figure out what aspect of the goddess you are calling upon and which goddess you would like to work with. Decorate the space with that goddess' favorite color, flower or scent.
- Do ethical work.
- Speak the name of the goddess.
- Remove karmic debt.

The ancient secret ways are available to everyone now. As you increase your unconditional love, receive guidance from your highest self and co-create through Divine will, your life becomes more powerful.

## Fairy Realm

If you were at a multicultural gathering and looking for a common interest to discuss with participants, fairies or nature spirits would be a good choice. Most countries and cultures have their own stories and myths surrounding fairies or nature spirits. They may be called elves, gnomes, pixies, brownies, forest nymphs, or assorted other names. And while each culture may interpret them a bit differently, the mission of the fairy realm is the same: they are nature spirits and the guardians of nature. Because of their dedication to Mother Earth, we tend to refer to fairies in the feminine although they are gender neutral.

Fairies inspire growth, encourage true presence and support love. It is said that when the earth was first created, the fairy realm existed. They are the overseers of everything in nature—they paint it, nurture it and help it grow. It is said there is a fairy for every flower, bush, tree, and blade of grass.

As humans evolved on earth, changes and damage occurred. Because of this, there is a rift between the fairies and us. Human beings have injured the fairy world as well as the earth. There has to be an effective communication and utilization of powers. What now needs to happen is for the fairy realm and humans to work together to restore and enhance the earth. Each cannot heal it alone, but together we can. Both human beings and the fairy realm have something unique and extraordinary to offer.

Acknowledging, praising and asking permission is very important to the fairy realm. Pay homage to the beauty of what they have created. Fairies understand the concept of change and evolution but require praise and acknowledgement. If you are going to change something on your property, ask their permission. Take a lesson from the Native Americans who asked permission and forgiveness of the tree they were about to chop down. They always took time to pay homage to the fairies and left behind a symbolic thank you of corn, tobacco or such. Fairies love to be acknowledged and appreciate gifts.

Fairies have their own distinct personalities and can be spontaneous. Working with the fairy realm can be joyful and empowering. Fairies are brilliant folk. Once you open the door to the faerie realm, you must use your highest self and your integrity. As always, follow the code of ethics.

Fairies have their own agendas. You are in a trance when you work with them so be clear about your goals. If you are not sure exactly who you are dealing with, you can always check it out by asking, "Are you of the Divine?" Say this three times and then ask, "Are you of the Divine plan?" another three times.

When you meditate, the veil between dimensions becomes thinner and you can go into the fairy dimension. You have to slow down to enter the fairies' kingdom. An added benefit of slowing down is that many things that you may not have noticed before will suddenly become beautiful. As you quiet yourself, your vibration changes on a physical, mental, emotional and spiritual level.

This vibration will bring you into harmony with nature. Your body can begin to change—for the better. You will feel more refreshed. Have you ever noticed how refreshed people look after they have spent some time in nature? It's a result of harmonizing with the fairy kingdom and the vibration of the enchantment realm.

The fairy kingdom exists in "between times"—such as dusk (between day and night), noon (between morning and afternoon), the edge of the forest and such. The best time for viewing fairies is midsummer eve at dusk, especially if the moon is full.

Fairies adore praise and appreciation. They need to be respected, honored and to have nature treated in a respectful, loving way.

Fairies encourage the pleasure principle. Notice the relationship of your physical body and emotions. Are you aware of your feelings and understand them or ignore them? Notice the small things that please you.

Fairies are aligned with one of the earth elements. Therefore, gnomes are related to the earth, undines are related to the water, sylphs are related to air and salamanders are related to fire.

**The fairies have a message: Preserve the environment.** The key to working with the fairy realm is to understand the interconnectedness of the earth. Growth is a never-ending process and we are all in this together. Everyone and everything are part of everyone and everything else. No matter where you are in life, you are still involved in the process and have the ability to grow.

It will take both the fairy realm and humans to channel our growth in a positive way for the environment. One woman who communicated with the fairies made some life-style adjustments to help preserve the environment. She recommends composting kitchen scraps and yard waste and using the compost to fertilize your flower and shrub beds. Shred yard leaves in the fall to cover flower and shrub beds. It keeps weeds down and provides a nourishing soil enhancement. Do not use chemical fertilizers on the lawn. Many fairies are sensitive to it and the chemicals filter into our water system.

Finally, Walk, walk, walk. Cut down on vehicle emissions, gas consumption and get exercise at the same time. Perhaps the biggest benefit of walking is it gets you closer to the fairy realm, nature and all of the magic associated with it.

## Spirit Guides

A spirit guide is a presence of energy that vibrates at a high and particular frequency of unconditional love. As you move to a higher vibration and become more aware, you can tap into these guides because they are here to help you. There are many categories of spirit guides and some of them include:

- ☐ Angel
- ☐ Ancestor
- ☐ Animal totem
- ☐ Archangel
- ☐ Ascended master
- ☐ Goddess and God
- ☐ Fairy
- ☐ Reiki
- ☐ Saints
- ☐ Seichim

Each presence has a special connection and purpose for your life. You may find there are often things that "pull" you in different directions to people, places and events. As you meditate and bring yourself into the vibration of peace, harmony and unconditional love, you become more aware of this presence as a source of help to you. Also, working with guides can accelerate your growth.

Spirit guides come out of grace to give you information to help you stay on your Divine path moment to moment. You may be able to see them out of the corner of your eye or they might appear as a mist. Have you ever looked at your newly developed pictures and wondered why there was a cloudy mist in the picture? Take a closer look; chances are it's a spirit guide.

Depending on your gifts and sensitivities you will receive the information either inside or outside of you. You may also hear, see or feel them depending on your own special talents. Help from spirit guides can come in ordinary ways. Perhaps it's a sudden hunch, inspiration or inner voice that gives you a solution. Or it could be a chance meeting, a suggestion from a friend or unexpected change of plans that help get you moving in the right direction.

In the beginning you can use meditation to take you to a golden corridor and locate a doorway with your name. Go in and experience what emerges from the edges. Perhaps the guide has a gift, symbol or information for you. Receive the gift with appreciation and ask any questions you have. You can ask the guide to return with you to your daily life if you like.

If you would like to see your guides, go into meditation facing a mirror with a plain wall behind you. Stare at your forehead for 60 seconds while relaxing and meditating. Ask to see the highest Divine guide working with you now according to your Divine purposes. Look to the side of you for an after image. Watch the after image change shapes. As the image fades, look back to your forehead then to your sides for more shapes.

At another time you can ask your guardian angel to do things for you as long as you respect the free choice of others and your own Divine path. We all have free wills and a true guide will never make decisions for you, even if you ask. Remember that if a guide is telling you what to do or if it doesn't feel like unconditional love, ask it three times, "Are you of the Divine?" Then ask three more times "Are you of the Divine purpose?" Anything that is not for your Divine purpose will fade and it is wise to let it go.

The more you work with guides, the more information will unfold. You will learn about the realms they assist in and how to utilize their energies to increase your success in manifesting love, work and health.

## Sacred Sites

Sacred sites are places where the consciousness of other times exists. Energy at sacred sites radiates at a higher frequency than other areas, and offers visitors an accelerated experience and opportunity for deep spiritual evolution. Sacred sites provide the potential for tapping into information, and balancing and healing. Sites have energy that can help us to understand more about ourselves which is beneficial for self-discovery. When you visit a sacred site you can tap into the vibration of truth and often can experience more information from your highest self.

Many sacred sites are like chakras in that they are the chakras of the earth. People from all over the world are attracted to these sites because of the amazing occurrences that can take place there. Examples of well known sacred sites are in Sedona, Macchu Pichu, Stonehenge and Easter Island, to name just a few.

But sacred sites can exist right down the street from you, often in the form of former Native American habitats or nature. Often bodies of water, forests, deserts and other aspects of nature contain the properties of sacred sites. Students can learn to use meditation and telepathy to contact ancient spirits and all their knowledge.

## Grokking

In his science fiction book *Stranger in a Strange Land*,

Robert Heinlein used the word "grok" to describe a technique used by Martians to understand the world and people around them. Grokking involved communing on such a fundamental level that understanding transcends language and is felt more than described.

Grokking, as we use the term, is a kahuna method that increases psychic abilities. Everything (person, place or thing) has a spirit and you can communicate with it. It could be a sacred site, Lemurian crystal, a rock, mummy, etc. Start by imagining yourself becoming very small. Imagine yourself traveling to the center of the object. Communicate telepathically with the object. Follow this process in preparing to grok:

1. Ask if the object is willing to work with you.
2. Ask permission to speak.
3. If you have permission, ask it anything or let it talk to you.
4. Tell it how much you appreciate this opportunity to interact with it.
5. Ask what it wants from you.
6. Ask what it can teach you.

When you grok you get answers to your questions and a sense of what is true. But be sure you have permission.

***Exercise 10A: Goddess.*** Indicate which of the following energies are emerging in your life at this time. The goddess can evoke many different feelings and responses in people. In the following chart indicate which of the following energies are emerging in your life at this time. You may want to measure these over time to determine the changes that are taking place in your life.

|  | CREATION | BIRTH | DEATH | REBIRTH | TRANSFORMATION | RESTORATION | NURTURANCE | HEALING | INTUITION | TRUTH | TEACHING | MAGIC | WISDOM |
|---|---|---|---|---|---|---|---|---|---|---|---|---|---|
| NONEXISTENT | ○ | ○ | ○ | ○ | ○ | ○ | ○ | ○ | ○ | ○ | ○ | ○ | ○ |
| SELDOM THERE | ○ | ○ | ○ | ○ | ○ | ○ | ○ | ○ | ○ | ○ | ○ | ○ | ○ |
| HALF THERE | ○ | ○ | ○ | ○ | ○ | ○ | ○ | ○ | ○ | ○ | ○ | ○ | ○ |
| MOSTLY THERE | ○ | ○ | ○ | ○ | ○ | ○ | ○ | ○ | ○ | ○ | ○ | ○ | ○ |
| ALWAYS THERE | ○ | ○ | ○ | ○ | ○ | ○ | ○ | ○ | ○ | ○ | ○ | ○ | ○ |

|  | FRIENDSHIP | PROTECTION | LOVE | ATTRACTION | SEXUALITY | CELEBRATION | WORSHIP | PRAYER | DIVINITY | LOVING | CREATIVE EXPRESSION | GARDENING | ART |
|---|---|---|---|---|---|---|---|---|---|---|---|---|---|
| NONEXISTENT | ○ | ○ | ○ | ○ | ○ | ○ | ○ | ○ | ○ | ○ | ○ | ○ | ○ |
| SELDOM THERE | ○ | ○ | ○ | ○ | ○ | ○ | ○ | ○ | ○ | ○ | ○ | ○ | ○ |
| HALF THERE | ○ | ○ | ○ | ○ | ○ | ○ | ○ | ○ | ○ | ○ | ○ | ○ | ○ |
| MOSTLY THERE | ○ | ○ | ○ | ○ | ○ | ○ | ○ | ○ | ○ | ○ | ○ | ○ | ○ |
| ALWAYS THERE | ○ | ○ | ○ | ○ | ○ | ○ | ○ | ○ | ○ | ○ | ○ | ○ | ○ |

The goddess can evoke many different feelings and responses in people. Indicate which of the following energies are emerging in your life at this time.
You may want to measure these over time to determine the changes that are taking place.

*12 – Goddess Energy Map*

**Exercise 10B: Fairy.** Do one small action every day that is pleasing to you. Sit by a beautiful plant, spend an hour in the garden. No hurrying. Do not rush from one step to the other trying to get to the next one. Relax. Ask the fairies to help you. They are eager to see everyone participate in the pleasure principal.

**Exercise 10C: Spirit guides.** As you get to know your guides you may come to a place in your life where you want their energy within you all the time. This exercise will help you to do that.

1. Go into meditation and image the guide standing in front of you.
2. Ask your highest self for permission to integrate the energy within you.
3. If OK, ask the guide for permission.
4. Step into the guide energy and feel the shifts.
5. Look back at your old energy and send it to the center of the earth to be processed according the Divine will.

# CHAPTER 15

## *Past Life Experiences*

Past life issues may reveal themselves when a person experiences blocks, fears, phobias, pain or other things that are not rational or explainable. Participating in a past life regression can be extremely useful to understand more about yourself, release blocks and help you actualize your potential.

The phenomenon is mysterious in that it may come from unknown sources, actual past life experiences or you may be carrying the burden of humanity by tapping into the all-knowing unconscious. Perhaps the best way to work with it is to not judge the phenomenon, but to use it in a therapeutic way.

People who remember a past life experience feel that it is not a dream but something that happened. It may have really happened to that person or he or she may be tapping into the all-knowing unconscious.

A person goes under hypnosis to access hidden memories. As the person remembers the past life experience, he or she can therapeutically explore the effect that the past life has had on the present life. When those memories become conscious, they have much less power to block the person and interfere. Much stress is released. Past life healing can help on a physical, mental, emotional and spiritual level.

Through past life regression, people often realize that the way they feel about something today is not based on what has taken place in this life. A past life regression can also clear karmic debts and help you realize your wonderful positive strengths.

## Who Should Have a Past Life Regression?

People with pain that does not respond to conventional treatment are good candidates for past life regression work. Some pain is said to be in the aura level of a past life. For example, a runner with sciatica did a past life regression and the pain went away. You find people with back or knee pain that is particularly relevant to something that has occurred, or they feel occurred, in a past life.

People often go through a past life regression when they feel stuck. It is a very freeing experience. Often people will do a past life regression to gain a deeper understanding of themselves. Some people do it out of curiosity. If you are considering doing a past life regression, ask yourself:

- Do you have any images in your mind that are not dreams or experiences in this life?
- Do you ever feel déjà vu in a location or with certain people you meet?
- Do you have any physical pain not explained by occurrences in this life?
- Do you have emotional pain or fear not explained in this life?
- Do you have any spontaneous visions or flashbacks not explained in this life?

Resolving past life issues that are real or imagined has a

very positive effect on an individual's everyday life and functioning.

## When to Do a Past Life Regression

It is very important that you have some stability and clarity with this life before you begin to confuse or frustrate yourself with a past life. A good starting point is to take a meditation class until you are ready. The class will also help you access information much easier.

A word of caution: Always work with an experienced, certified professional hypnotherapist. The information that surfaces needs to be reframed in a realistic way and put into the context of your current life. A professional can help interpret the information and find the relevance of your feelings and the things that are happening to you in this life.

## More Examples

One woman did a past life regression to discover she was a goddess in a past era and had total love and devotion. Her problem was she could not achieve the same feeling in this life. When she realized that she was actually grieving a loss of these feelings, she was able to complete the grieving process, bring her energies into the now and focus on the love and devotion she has in this life.

Another woman who did a past life regression was having a difficult time interacting with her co-workers. In her regression she lived in western times. She was abandoned but found by a band of wonderful people who cared for and nurtured her. They saved her life and she was totally connected to them and lived out her life in that environment. However, her problem in this life was she was not able to find that connection working in the corporate world. Once she realized what was happening, she was able to connect with her work group because she could let go of that unconscious ideal and begin again where she was in this life.

There are many similar examples. Past life work can be a component in a series of steps to get you centered, balanced and focused. Once you know what your callings are, you can begin to work on them with total commitment. You can let go of the history and work on the here and now to fulfill your hopes and dreams.

The more you remove the negatives and understand the positives, the more it can benefit you. Once these blocks are understood and treated, you can better know your callings and purposes and go after them proactively. Finally, the rate of healing that takes place after a past life regression can be accelerated.

# CHAPTER 16

## *Parts of Yourself*

A cornerstone of Integration Psychology is that people no longer need to go outside themselves for answers but they can find the answers within themselves. To do this it's helpful for you to identify and understand the different parts of yourself and then to get them working synergistically. When there is agreement, laser-sharp focus and empowerment occur.

Integration is about accepting the different parts of your self. We are taught that certain aspects of our selves are not acceptable. In fact, moment to moment, all aspects of our selves are needed for us to be who we are at any given time.

## Name your Parts

In Chapter 4 we discussed the purpose of the highest self, ego and feelings. In addition to these three, there are many different parts functioning within you. The following is a list of the more common parts that people often describe about themselves. You have these parts within you and there may be additional parts that you can identify. The following are some suggestions to help you identify you own parts.

- **Adult**—Your rational, responsible self.
- **Body, astral**—The ethereal body double of the physical body.
- **Body, physical**—The integrity of the physical body.
- **Chakras**—The energy vortex centers that channel emotional, physical and spiritual energy throughout the system.
- **Conscious mind**—The part of you that is aware in the here and now, moment to moment.
- **Ego**—The information center that tells you what is happening on the earth plane with regard to how you are doing in earth matters and how others are relating to you.
- **Ethereal**—Vital life force found in your aura.
- **Feelings**—Feelings may be pathologic or healthy. Pathological feelings are destructive and disturbing; they float around and are not connected to anything specific that is happening to you in the moment. These feelings are generated by someone else and projected onto you or they are feelings that have been building up over time and have not been dealt with. Healthy feelings are an energy that get our attention and give us information about anything and everything. When properly acknowledged, the feeling will naturally dissipate.
- **Gender identity**—Your self-concept related to your male/female condition.
- **Highest self**—Your highest self is an exten-

sion of your soul and is a spiritual bridge between your earth existence and your total Divine self. Your highest self is earth-related and its purpose is to keep you on your Divine path. Your highest self knows what you are supposed to be doing moment to moment. It has any answer you need.
- *Identity*—The aspects of earth existence you actualize in yourself and in your life. This is how you integrate your culture, gender, etc.
- *Inner child*—The child part of you usually located in your sacral chakra in the lower abdomen.
- *Inner critic*—The energy voice within that critiques you.
- *Non-personal Divine*—Located above your highest self and is the connection to the Divine source that is connected to all.
- *Other*—Any other parts that you discover within you.
- *Parent*—The part that parents you and your inner child.
- *Personality*—Your mental style of handling life. This style has many qualities such as being an extrovert or introvert.
- *Soul*—The spiritual core of an individual. It is intense Divine love and retains the information and wisdom that travels from and into infinity.
- *Spirit*—Divine essence in various vibrations and forms to serve the highest power here on earth and elsewhere in the universe.
- *Temperament*—The coping and adjusting qualities brought into your life at birth.
- *Thoughts*—Mental activity at the brain and

mind level.

- **Unconscious Mind**—The part of your mind that stores feelings and memories. Your conscious mind is not aware of everything stored in your unconscious mind.

You have these parts within you and there may be additional parts that you can identify. Think about what these might be named and identify what they do.

Internal conflict is necessary and when it is resolved, you will function at a higher level. When you are on the path and work hard to achieve your dream, you will have a sense of achievement, satisfaction, accomplishment and closure.

To accomplish your Divine mission, you must utilize and integrate the parts of yourself just like a well-coordinated team. This process involves the following steps:

1. Communicate to the different parts of yourself.
2. Discover conflicts and strengths.
3. Resolve conflicts.
4. Function as a team guided by your highest self.

**Exercise 11A: Parts of yourself chart: Identify the parts of yourself.** Use the charts on the next pages to identify the different parts of yourself.

**Exercise 11B: Parts of yourself chart: How are you working as a team?** Use the charts on the next pages to document how the different parts of yourself are working together at this time and to identify which parts need more integration.

|  | ADULT | BODY - ASTRAL | BODY - PHYSICAL | CHAKRAS | CONSCIOUS MIND | EGO | ETHEREAL | FEELINGS | GENDER IDENTITY | HIGHEST SELF | IDENTITY |
|---|---|---|---|---|---|---|---|---|---|---|---|
| NONEXISTENT | ○ | ○ | ○ | ○ | ○ | ○ | ○ | ○ | ○ | ○ | ○ |
| SELDOM THERE | ○ | ○ | ○ | ○ | ○ | ○ | ○ | ○ | ○ | ○ | ○ |
| HALF THERE | ○ | ○ | ○ | ○ | ○ | ○ | ○ | ○ | ○ | ○ | ○ |
| MOSTLY THERE | ○ | ○ | ○ | ○ | ○ | ○ | ○ | ○ | ○ | ○ | ○ |
| ALWAYS THERE | ○ | ○ | ○ | ○ | ○ | ○ | ○ | ○ | ○ | ○ | ○ |

|  | INNER CHILD | INNER CRITIC | NON-PERSONAL DIVINE | OTHER | PARENT | PERSONALITY | SOUL | SPIRIT | TEMPERAMENT | THOUGHTS | UNCONSCIOUS MIND |
|---|---|---|---|---|---|---|---|---|---|---|---|
| NONEXISTENT | ○ | ○ | ○ | ○ | ○ | ○ | ○ | ○ | ○ | ○ | ○ |
| SELDOM THERE | ○ | ○ | ○ | ○ | ○ | ○ | ○ | ○ | ○ | ○ | ○ |
| HALF THERE | ○ | ○ | ○ | ○ | ○ | ○ | ○ | ○ | ○ | ○ | ○ |
| MOSTLY THERE | ○ | ○ | ○ | ○ | ○ | ○ | ○ | ○ | ○ | ○ | ○ |
| ALWAYS THERE | ○ | ○ | ○ | ○ | ○ | ○ | ○ | ○ | ○ | ○ | ○ |

The goal is to identify and understand the different parts of yourself and to get them working together.

### 13 – Identifying Parts of Yourself

| | ADULT | BODY - ASTRAL | BODY - PHYSICAL | CHAKRAS | CONSCIOUS MIND | EGO | ETHEREAL | FEELINGS | GENDER IDENTITY | HIGHEST SELF | IDENTITY |
|---|---|---|---|---|---|---|---|---|---|---|---|
| LONER | ○ | ○ | ○ | ○ | ○ | ○ | ○ | ○ | ○ | ○ | ○ |
| SOMETIMES | ○ | ○ | ○ | ○ | ○ | ○ | ○ | ○ | ○ | ○ | ○ |
| TEAM PLAYER | ○ | ○ | ○ | ○ | ○ | ○ | ○ | ○ | ○ | ○ | ○ |

| | INNER CHILD | INNER CRITIC | NON-PERSONAL DIVINE | OTHER | PARENT | PERSONALITY | SOUL | SPIRIT | TEMPERAMENT | THOUGHTS | UNCONSCIOUS MIND |
|---|---|---|---|---|---|---|---|---|---|---|---|
| LONER | ○ | ○ | ○ | ○ | ○ | ○ | ○ | ○ | ○ | ○ | ○ |
| SOMETIMES | ○ | ○ | ○ | ○ | ○ | ○ | ○ | ○ | ○ | ○ | ○ |
| TEAM PLAYER | ○ | ○ | ○ | ○ | ○ | ○ | ○ | ○ | ○ | ○ | ○ |

*The goal is to identify and understand the different parts of yourself and to get them working together.*

**14 – Determining Teamwork Between Parts of Yourself**

***Exercise 11C—Parts of yourself.*** Take a problem or an issue you are dealing with in this life and try to figure out what part (or parts) of you is/are creating the problem.

1. Think about something in your life that is not working or you would like to see improved.
2. Scan your body with your mind and determine if you can sense this in your physical body.
3. Scan your emotions.
4. Scan your thoughts.

5. Write down what you find.
6. Go inside yourself and ask where the beginning of this started.
7. Ask what parts of you are involved. Once identified, speak to each part and find out what it wants you to know.
8. Ask yourself what the goal is and how to coordinate the parts now and in the future.

Spend the next week paying attention to the various parts of your self and determine where you are in the self-mastery flow cycle as discussed in Chapter 3. Only make changes through the guidance of your highest self.

# PART IV

# Self Mastery Through Integration

# CHAPTER 17

## *Healing and Manifesting on the Astral Plane*

The ultimate technique to create the life you desire is going to the astral plane. The astral plane is a real place of being and awareness. Only after an idea or feeling is placed on the astral plane, can it materialize on the earth plane. For example, before an artist creates a painting or a sculpture, the idea of that work of art already has form in the astral before it is made tangible on earth. A phenomenon exists on the astral plane through imagination, visualization, intention and felt emotion. This chapter teaches you to go to the astral plane through your imagination.

By using this method, two things become much more powerful on the earth plane: healing and manifesting. Healing is bringing the mental, emotional, spiritual and physical into balance. Manifesting is making your hopes and dreams become a reality. These can be accomplished by using the astral plane. To manifest your desires, create them on the astral plane, imagine them in your mind, take proper action and they will appear on the earth plane.

The astral plane also offers the opportunity to gain information and empower your intentions. Practice on a regular basis because the more you do it, the more power you develop. The more you open yourself to the astral plane, the greater your success.

When you are working on the astral plane you are also working with the unconscious mind, and sometimes your belief system gets in the way. As we've discussed, there's a difference between what we believe and what we know. We hold onto our beliefs until we know something for sure as discussed in Chapter 2. Through meditation and travel to the astral plane, you can become aware of your own truth and universal truths. A universal truth is something that is true for most people and is something they agree with, can relate to and resonate with.

## Astral Travel

The way to get to the astral plane is through astral travel. Astral travel is purposefully separating your astral body from your physical body and sending it to the astral plane. The astral body is your consciousness and it goes with you from one lifetime to the next. It is connected to you through a silver cord. Only people who are balanced and healthy should attempt to astral travel.

The benefits to astral travel are that it:

- Increases creativity.
- Develops intuition and psychic abilities.
- Manipulates time.
- Increases manifesting abilities.
- Reduces stress.
- Strengthens healing energies.
- Promotes better health.
- Improves concentration and memory.
- Connects with your highest self.
- Taps into the all-knowing unconsciousness.
- Strengthens balancing.

- Enhances confidence and happiness.
- Increases spirituality.

During astral travel you can communicate with anyone on the astral plane—past, present or future. It could be Freud, Jung or Einstein as well as your ancestors. You can be anywhere in your mind in time.

Sometimes it is not so much what happens when you are on the astral plane as what happens to you when you get back and over subsequent days. Astral travel allows you to find out who you are and your core truths of life. The issues you are dealing with and sorting out help to determine what you are committed to. You may get answers to questions you didn't know you had. Also, information can spontaneously come to you.

In astral travel truths emerge and you may see where you want to be stronger and support some aspect of yourself to get further in your dreams and hopes. As discussed in the flow of self mastery, there may be some uncomfortable moments as you get closer to the truth.

The colors on the astral plane are very interesting and not like earth colors. You may have a black or purple background. Colors may not really blend. For example, although yellow and green make blue, you may see a combination of both yellow and green without it being blue.

When you first travel and return to your body it can be a jolt. It might be like when you are falling asleep and jump. You might experience vibrations or sounds. It is normal for people to have different experiences. There is no record of anyone going to the astral plane and not returning. Often it's more difficult to stay out as people keep returning to their body when they would rather be on the astral plane.

## Ground Training and Suggestions

The easiest way to astral travel is through visualization and imagination. We are moving to the fifth dimension where you think something and it quickly appears. The more you practice astral travel, the better you get and the more interesting it becomes. The goal is to increase the energy.

Before you attempt astral travel, there are some ground training practices and suggestions that may be helpful for you to know. These include:

- **Health concerns:** People with heart conditions, mental problems or seizure disorders should not participate in astral travel without the consent of a physician.
- **Breathing:** Practice vibrational breathing which is similar to what yoga practitioners call *ujjayi* (ooh-jah-yee) breathing or throat breathing. Vibrational breathing is done by making a slight humming noise when breathing. Try it first on an exhale breath then try it while inhaling. Finally connect your throat and middle eye. Practice this connection for several minutes at a time. Make the third eye vibrate the same as the throat.
- **Travel vehicle:** Practice having your astral body leave your body as a mist and turn it into a vehicle or form that you can travel in. You might want to imagine your astral body in a different shape than your physical body.
- **Method of leaving the body:** Your astral body can leave the physical body through the solar plexus or the crown chakra. Release a mix of your energy from your crown chakra or solar plexus chakra or peel your astral energy from your body.

- **Silver Cord:** Your astral body is attached to your physical body by a silver cord. If you need to come back, you can. Pull on your silver cord and immediately return to the earth plane. While leaving the body or throughout astral travel, people sometimes shake, hear different sounds such as rushing water or are jarred back into their bodies.
- **Protection:** With your intention, place protection around all parts of your self. Take a symbol of protection with you and wrap a bubble of peace around your physical and astral bodies. Some people use crosses, Reiki symbols or anything that means protection for them. Take your highest Divine spirit guide. Use the affirmation, "Only good will come to me and only good will leave from me now."
- **Ethics:** Ethics are critical. Your work becomes much more powerful when ethics are practiced. Two of the most important ethical points are permission and intention. First, obtain permission by verbally asking for it. Ask for permission (May I, should I, can I do this?). Don't visit places you have no business to be in (homes, bedrooms, etc.). Only go where you have permission. Second, intention is most important. Take it seriously and use intentions purposefully.

## Negative Experiences

You may wonder about negative or frightening things happening. If you think of something bad, will it happen? Fears or anxieties don't necessarily create negative experiences but more often create blocks. If negative thoughts or blocks occur, ask your highest self why this is happening. Another way to deal with it is to apply affirmations. For example say, "The best possible is happening now."

There is a universal law and if you are approached by something you are not sure of, ask "Are you of the Divine?" three times. Then ask again "Are you of the Divine purpose?" three times. Or say "God" six times. If it is not of the Divine, it will go away. You are always safe as long as you are practicing while being in the white light. And remember, if you can make it up, you can make it go away!

When you are of the white light, love and of good intention, you will always have more power than anything negative. If you come upon something negative, realize your own power and you can ward it away permanently.

## Bi-locating and Grounding

Often when people go to the astral plane, they begin bi-locating or become aware of being in two places at once. For example, you are aware of your physical body on the earth plane while you are visualizing and imagining on the astral plane.

Some people bi-locate and don't realize it. It's possible to be on the astral plane without your planning or conscious awareness of it. If you blank out a lot or experience a loss of time, you are probably not grounded. So it is important to ground yourself. Hematite is an excellent grounding stone. Refer to grounding information discussed in Chapter 5. Determine what technique will work best for you to ground and connect to the earth.

Also, a lot of people go to the astral plane to escape. However, this can create problems because you are not emotionally in your body and can have accidents, get sick, blank out and not know what is going on.

## Vibration Layers

On the astral plane there are different layers of vibration and those layers vary from the highest positive of all to the most horribly negative. Your mood will determine which level you will access. The mood you are in when you leave the earth plane will follow you to the astral plane. So don't travel if you are in a bad mood, don't feel well or are worried or angry about something.

Emotion is automatically placed on the astral plane. Therefore, whatever you are feeling, be it depression, rage or love, it will be manifested in your life. Whatever you think about, feel and intend starts to manifest on the earth plane as a real situation. Astral travel is most powerful when you put a feeling on the astral plane. You can use it for manifesting feelings of love, peace and harmony. If you imagine something on the astral plane, your unconscious will bring it to you.

## Sleep and Travel

When you sleep you naturally travel to the astral plane. About 15 minutes before you go to sleep, get into a calm, peaceful mood because the mood you are in before you go to sleep determines the layer of the astral plane you go to. If you are vibrating in love, trust and harmony before sleep, that is the level you go to while sleeping. If you watch the news filled with violence, you vibrate at stress, fear and negativity and that is the level you go to during sleep.

You can override all that by asking your Divine guide to take you to a peaceful, harmonious place and keep you safe throughout the night. It never hurts to have crosses and protective symbols around your bed.

## Akashic Records

The Akashic Records are the library of everything that has been thought, done, felt or said in the past, present or future by each soul. They are located on the layer next to the astral plane. Through the Akashic Records, you can obtain information, adjust karmic debts and change destiny. This should only be done using the highest ethics.

A powerful way to impact your life through the Akashic Records is to make affirmations. Affirmations speak directly to your unconscious mind and have the power to change things instantly. As discussed, positive affirmations are a good way to manifest the things you want.

## Tips/Thoughts About Astral Travel

To have the ultimate experience with astral travel, you must have balance in your physical, emotional and spiritual self. The following promote a positive experience:

1. Astral travel is best done if you are calm and in good health. Sensitivity helps to increase astral travel abilities.
2. When traveling, make sure you have a quiet, secure environment as you do when meditating. Don't have pets or the phone around for distractions.
3. Imagine and visualize a healing, sacred place to travel to. When you go to that place, use affirmations that will be very positive for you.
4. It's best not to eat or drink a couple of hours before travel as it is easier for chakras to open and allow you to travel more effectively. A travel diet (high vibrational diet) includes lots of fresh fruits and vegetables (particularly car-

rots), no meat and very little chicken and fish. If you feel too jittery or buzzy, one way to ground is to eat meat or dairy products. Brown rice is the most centering of foods.
5. Strengthen your body so it can match your mind. Physical exercise is good and gives you more prana and chi.
6. Go outside and be within nature.
7. The vibration of the stone, iolite, can help you travel.
8. After you return, call back all of your energy and reintegrate it into yourself. When you astral travel and it benefits your earth existence, then you are successful.

## The Will Technique

Doing astral travel at will is simply willing that your astral body travel to a specific spot. This is one of the easiest techniques to use. Your Divine will is in the solar plexus and is the color yellow.

Imagine increasing the energy in your solar plexus. If you make your will strong enough, you can do many things. Ask your highest self for permission and help. This will strengthen your Divine will. Practice using your Divine will and self-confidence. Focus your mind and intentions to achieve success. Without your Divine will, purpose and confidence, success will be difficult.

**Check sheet**: Here's a step-by-step summary guide to travel:

- ♦ Relax: Get into a relaxed vibration. Make sure your space won't be interrupted.
- ♦ Protection: Determine what and who you will take.
- ♦ Silver cord: Be aware of your silver cord.
- ♦ Breathing: Use the breathing technique that works best for you.

- Meditate: Bring earth energy in through your feet and feel the vibration. Bring the energy up through all your chakras. Bring sky energy in through your crown chakra and integrate the sky and earth energy.
- Vibrate: Purposely vibrate each part of your body. Separate your astral energy from your physical body.
- Travel to your location: Take your astral body to the location you have identified.
- Be grateful: Thank your astral plane guides as they greet you. Ask what information they have for you. You may have a gift for them. Show your appreciation before you leave.
- Return: Come back to your physical body: Call back all energy from the past, present and future to your physical body and re-integrate it.
- Bubble of peace: Place a bubble of peace around your body.
- Ground yourself: Stomp your feet three times or use other techniques.

## Side Effects

Healing is bringing the mental, emotional, spiritual and physical into balance. While the rewards of healing are great, you may experience some unusual or unpleasant side effects while doing the work to achieve balance. In this work you increase your vital life force. When vital life force increases, blocks are eliminated and channels are widened. Symptoms include:

- Emotional: Swings in emotions are not uncommon. One moment you may be flying high and the next you are in the depths of depression. Also bursts of anger and tears seem to come from nowhere. Spontaneous crying or laughing can be a sign of healing. Irritation emerges as the emotions are being released. Issues from your past come up from your consciousness and then fade. Issues that stay longer than four days should be addressed.

- Physical: Flu-like symptoms, muscle aches and pains and nausea may also be experienced. If you had a previous illness, you may feel some of the symptoms that were associated with that illness. Specific and unusual tastes can occur in your mouth. Body odors may emerge.
- Psychic phenomena: This can range from hunches that are almost always right to precognitive dreams. Pay attention to the way you receive psychic impressions so you can better understand and enhance what works for you.

  - Clairvoyance: Your inner vision. This is the ability to visualize an image as it appears in the past, present or future. Auric sight refers to the ability to view auras.
  - Clairaudience: Your inner voice. This is the ability to hear sounds that aren't accessible to the physical ear. This could be sounds such as voices, music or ringing.
  - Clairsentience: Your inner sensing the feelings of others. This is the ability to perceive things out of the range of ordinary perception. It's the things you know, but don't know how you know.

Other side affects are discussed in Chapter 4 (detoxification and shutting down of your highest self and psychic abilities) and in Chapter 7 (physical changes).

# CHAPTER 18

## *Integration Psychology*

When you connect to your highest self and direct your energy, the universe opens up to you. Amazing transformations take place with people who follow the steps. This book has laid the groundwork for the basic steps; now you can continue to grow and integrate them.

### Co-creation

One of the most beneficial things that happen with this work is co-creation. It occurs when you listen to your highest self, which knows your callings and purposes here on earth. Being connected consciously to your highest self puts you in harmony with the creative forces of the universe, and can then allow for manifestation and miracles to enter your life.

For example, you might find yourself in a job that brings you financial security, but no real joy. In communicating with your highest self, you might be guided to change your employment and pursue another career that's important to you. The more you heed the intuitive guidance of your highest self, the more opportunities become available to you.

There are thousands of stories of people who managed to create the lives they wanted by seemingly miraculous coincidence. These are the people who are practicing co-creation—even if they don't know they are. All of the power to transform your life lies within you.

You want to move beyond the belief system to a knowing system. Through integration, the balance and strength of the body, mind and spirit work synergistically. A clarity of purpose moment to moment and for your ultimate destiny can then emerge. Know and use the methods outlined in this book to maintain your efficacies and become the master of your destiny. Good things will come to you.

## Moving to the Sixth Dimension

We are evolving through more effective energy vibrations of functioning. We refer to these as "dimensions." The word dimension comes from the Latin word *dimensio*, which means measuring. For the sake of differentiation, let's separate the different levels or dimensions. Although we can define each dimension, they do overlap.

**First Dimension**—The first measurement through a line; the shortest distance between two points.

**Second Dimension**—The second dimension emerges when a line or direction can be taken as an angle to the first flat plane or straight line. These lines can intersect, cross each another or fuse.

**Third Dimension**—The third dimension releases life from the flat surface to produce solid three-dimensional objects. It is a material dimension influenced by a cause and effect level where an individual functions with the idea of concrete, fixed quantities such as $1+1 = 2$.

When we talk of the third dimension, it also includes the first and second dimension. What's happened with the third dimension is the realization that humans can possess solid objects that can also be taken from them. The third dimension is really one of separatism as expressed by divisions and separations. This can lead to possessiveness, love of power and the inclination to take for yourself at the expense of others which can produce greed and fear.

**Fourth Dimension**—In the fourth dimension we comprehend that we are all connected and unified through a wave of energy. When we send something out it is received and then returns to us, forming a loop of energy. In the fourth dimension separatism transforms and opens to the channel of grace and abundance.

**Fifth Dimension**—The fifth dimension is the perception that each one of us is a universe and the universe exists inside ourselves. It allows for the transformation and transmutation of anything internally through the self which is then actualized outside the self. For example, when we think something at this level it occurs simultaneously.

**Sixth Dimension**—The sixth dimension is the complete integration of body, mind and spirit which then allows for materialization and dematerialization. This is travel through teleportation. Mystical people have been reported as being seen at two places at one time. This is the pinnacle of self mastery.

## The All-Knowing Unconscious

Carl Jung talked about the all-knowing unconscious and archetypes. When you go into meditation you can tap into the consciousness of anything that exists now, in the past or even in the future. Through meditation you can access the "all knowing unconscious." This is the bank of information that houses our total consciousness. So, if you want to know something, you have the power to access it if you know how and are well intended.

## Forging Forward on Your Path

Now that you have completed reading the book, begin to integrate the concepts through the use of meditation as a guide through the process. Realize where you are in the self-mastery ascension process. Use the highest of ethical standards and understand the law of karma to remove blocks.

Capture your ideas using a mind map and use a journal to track your progress. The pendulum and aura viewing can give you useful information. Use time manipulation, self-hypnosis and affirmations to help good things come to you. Understand the value of circles and their repeating cycles to benefit actions in your life.

Once you are using these techniques, you will probably begin having mystical experiences and be able to tap into more of the energies that are available to you. Utilize the strengths of the goddess, knowledge of the fairies, and other valuable insights you can gain through spirits, sacred sites and grokking.

Then, when you are ready, explore your past life experiences to gain a deeper understanding of yourself. Integrate all your parts and get them working together through the direction of your highest self, ego and feelings.

Finally you can go to the astral plane to heal and manifest your ultimate destiny and bring peace, love and harmony to the earth.

No matter what is going on in you life, the methods are still applicable. The more you meditate, the easier it is to tap into the zone and your own integrity to:

- Channel light and transmute negativity.
- Communicate with your highest self.
- Stay tuned to your destiny moment to moment.
- Live your hopes and dreams and bring in love, peace and harmony to the earth.
- Rely on faith and trust in the Divine process, particularly during difficult times.

This book was written to take you to a new dimension and knowing of your personal and universal truths, manifest your dreams and live a life of peace and joy. To get the most current information about sessions, classes, tapes and what Penny is discovering, visit her website at: www.pennyweaver.com.

# BIBLIOGRAPHY

Brennen, Barbara, *Hands of Light*, New York, Bantam Books, 1988

Guiley, Rosemary Ellen and Place, Robert Michael, *The Alchemical Tarot*, San Francisco, CA, Thorsons, 1995

LeShan, Lawrence, *How to Meditate*, New York, First Back Bay, 1999

*Michigan Today*, Fall 2001

Robertson, Robin, *Jungian Psychology*, York Beach, ME: Nicolas-Hayes, Inc.1992

Shewmaker, Diane Ruth, *All Love*, Beaverton, OR, Celestial Wellspring Publications, 1999

Spilsbury, Ariel and Bryner, Michael, *The Mayan Oracle Return Path to the Stars*, Santa Fe, NM, Bear & Company, 1992

Stein, Diane, *Essential Reiki*, Freedom, CA, The Crossing Press, Inc., 1995

Usui, Mikas and Petter, Frank Arjara, *The Original Reiki Handbook of Dr. Mikas Usui,* Lotus Press, Shangra-La, 1999

# INDEX

**Abundance**
  Channel of grace and 139
  Cooperation and 102
  Connecting to the source
    of through meditation
    48, 53, 57
  Law of 58
  Model of 24
  Universal 80
**Addiction 28**
**Affirmations**
  Akashic Records and 132
  Altering time with 80-81
  Commitment and 68
  Dealing with negativity
    and 130
  Definition of 82
  Exercise in developing 83-
    84, 86
  "Only good will come to
    me . . ." 54, 82
  No results from 83
  Self-hypnosis and 85
  Tapping into universal
    abundance with 80
  Value of positive 69, 83
  Value of relaxation with 81
**Akashic Records 57, 132**
**Alpha Waves 40**
**Altars 41, 102**
**Angels 57, 107**
**Animal Totems 57**
**Anxiety 28, 52**
**Ascension 101, 140**
  Process of 30, 35
**Astral Plane 125, 130-32**
**Astral Travel 126-28, 130**
  Meditations for 133-34
**Auras 48, 51, 76-77, 117**
  Exercise in viewing 78-79
**Authenticity 58**
**Bad Habits 84**
**Balance 46, 48, 53, 85**
**Beliefs 26-27, 126**
**Bi-locating 130**
**Blocks 31, 115**
  Karma and 140
  Past lives and 112
  Releasing 35, 134

145

Body Scan 41, 53-54, 85, 121
Breath
   Counting 49-50
   In meditation 42
Bubble of Peace 37, 47, 51, 85
Chakras 42-45, 47, 53, 117, 128
   Of the earth 108
   Opening 74
Chi 46
Circles 87, 102
Clairaudio 135
Clairsentient 135
Clairvoyant 100, 135
Co-creation 137-38
Competition 58
Contemplation 49
Confidentiality 56
Cooperation 58
Déjà vu 113
Depression 28
Destiny 57
Detoxification 35, 50
Diet 51, 77, 132
Dimensions 100, 138-39
Divine Purpose 29, 55, 130
Divine Source 24, 29, 53-55, 57
Divine Universal Energy 45
Dowsing 71
Dreams 29, 67-68, 70, 83, 100, 125
Earth Energy 46-47
Earth Plane 36, 54, 129

Ego 36, 116-17
Energy 76
Energy Flow 24, 45, 48, 74
Environment 105
Ethics 55, 129
Exercise 77, 105
Fairy 57, 103-06, 110, 140
Fantasies 29
Fears 28, 31-32, 113, 131
Feelings 36, 116-17, 119
Flow of Self-mastery 122, 139
Free Choice 57
Freedom 58
Goals 67, 83, 104, 122
God 24
Goddess 24, 57
   Energy 100-02
   Exercise and map 109-10
Grace 139
Gratitude 67, 134
Grokking 108-09
Grounding 38, 51, 54, 130, 134
Growth 66-67, 105-06
Harmony 25, 46, 48, 53, 131
Healing 125, 134-35
Hematite 51
Highest Self 60, 72, 116-17, 77, 99, 133
   Agreement with the unconscious 84
   Definition and purpose of 34

Exercise in communicating with 36-37
Goddess and 101
Guidance of 58, 66, 137
**Humanistic Values 58**
**Hypnosis 34, 112**
**Inner Child 118**
**Inner Critic 118**
**Integration 47, 119**
**Integration Psychology 23-24, 116, 137**
**Intention**
Importance of 56-57, 129
"Only good will come to me . . ." 37
Goddess and 101
Astral plane and 125, 133
**Intuition 67, 71, 100**
**Iolite 133**
**Jealousy 28**
**Journaling 38, 54, 66-70**
**Jung, Carl 127, 139**
**Kahuna 109**
**Karma 58, 84, 140**
**Karmic Debt 102, 113**
**Ki 24, 46**
**Knowing 26-27**
**Labyrinth 91-93**
**Life Force Energy 42**
**Loop Process 32-33**
**Log 54**
**Love 25, 57, 59, 100, 106**
**Mandalas 41, 87, 102**
**Manifesting 125**
**Medicine Wheel 93-95, 102**

**Meditation**
Blocks and 32, 35
Definition of 39
Fairy realm and 104
Guides and 106-07
Health benefits of 40
Keys to practice of 41-42
Kinds of 49-50
Mind mapping and 63-64
Mystical events and 99
Personal knowing from 27
Process of 47-48
Success with 53-54, 111, 114, 140
**Memories 99, 112, 119**
**Mind Map 63-66, 69**
**Mindfulness 39, 52**
**Money 40. 137**
**Mood 89, 131, 134-35**
**Moon 87, 89-91, 105**
**Mystical Experiences 99**
**National Center for Complementary and Alternative Medicine 40**
**Native Americans 108**
**Nature 104**
**Negative Experiences 46, 77, 129, 131**
**Negative Thinking 63, 77, 83, 129**
**Parts of Self 116**
**Past Life 112-115**
**Pendulum 71, 74-75**
**Permission**

Asking for Divine 133
Ethics when working on others 56, 77, 129
Fairies and 103
Grokking and 109
Journals and 69
Telepathic 59
**Personality 116**
**Pleasure 110**
**Positive Self-Talk 83-84**
**Prana 24, 46**
**Protection 133**
**Psychic 76, 126, 135**
**Psychic Viewing 78**
**Psychotherapy 114**
**Pyramid 60**
**Qi 24, 46**
**Qi Gong 50**
**Reiki 46, 57, 102**
**Sacred Sites 108**
**Sekhem-Seichim 46, 57, 102**
**Self-hypnosis 82-85**
**Side Effects 134, 136**
**Silver Cord 126, 129, 133**
**Smudging 78**
**Spirit Guides**
Contacting 106-108
Developing relationship with 57
Exercise with 111
In auras 76, 79
**Stone Circles 88-89**
**Stonehenge 88**
**Subliminal Influences 83**
**Supernatural Forces 106**

**Symbols 129, 131**
**Tai Chi 50**
**Taped Meditation 50**
**Telepathy 59, 60, 108**
**Theta Waves 40**
**Time 80**
**Unconscious mind 118, 126, 132**
**Universal Unconscious 112, 126, 139**
**Vibration Layers 131**
**Vibrational Breathing (Ujjuyi) 128**
**White Light 47, 101**
**Will Technique 133**
**www.pennyweaver.com 141**
**Yoga 50**
**Zen 52**